Before we start, a huge... **THANK YOU** for purchasing this book!

The idea of this project was to simplify and learn to tell you what you NEED to know in the easiest way possible with lots of visual pictures and diagrams to help you to truly Learn Kitesurfing Faster.

For you get the most value out of your purchase I have created some supporting content to help you learn kitesurfing faster so

you can have even more **fun** on the water...

Listen to the podcast Toms Kiteboarding Tips (on Apple and Spotify) and get a refresher on the way to the beach (and hopefully be entertained too!)

Follow Toms Kiteboarding Tips on Instagram and on Facebook for regular tips

Join the Learn Kitesurfing Faster Facebook group and get support from the community.

Please feel free to get in contact with me and ask any kitesurfing related question through Instagram / Facebook / email tom@tomskiteboardingtips.com

Visit www.tomskiteboardingtips.com and read the blog

Check out the Youtube channel
**Toms Kiteboarding Tips**

**Learn Kitesurfing Faster** is available on Audiobook format from Amazons Audible

**Learn Kitesurfing Faster** is available in French and German on Amazon

**Come and have a personal lesson or advanced coaching session with me in the ultimate Kitesurfing paradise that Im lucky enough to call home in the Turks and Caicos islands @thebigbluecollective**

Lastly huge THANK YOU to all the people who have taken the time to get in contact or have left a review over the years since this book was first published in 2017 also THANK YOU for all the 5 star reviews on Amazon as every single one are hugely appreciated

If you would be so kind to take a few moments of your precious time to leave a review on Amazon I would be eternally grateful as it really helps the book and all the other kitesurfing resources I have created to help more people practice safe and respectful kitesurfing as well as spreading more good vibes on the beach.

# Special thanks to all the following contributors

## Pro Kitesurfer contributors

Bruna Kajiya – World Freestyle Champion brunakajiya.com.br
Hannah Whitely – 3 x British champ hannahwhiteley.com bestkiteboarding.com
Jalou Langeree – KSP World Champion, jaloulangeree.com naish.com
Lyde Heckroodt – RRD Team rider, SA Wave Kitesurfing champion theshoresoflife.com
Moona Whyte – KSP Kitesurfing World Champion Cabrinhakites.com
Ruben Lenten – Red Bull King of the Air Champion, pioneer of the Megaloop len10.com
Aaron Hadlow - Five times world freestyle champion, two time champion of the Red Bull King of the Air and current highest jump ever aaronhadlow.com northkites.com
Kevin Langeree – World Freestyle Champion, Red Bull King of the Air Champion kevinlangeree.com naishkites.com
Lewis Crathern – Brigton Pier jumper, Professional Kitesurfer, British Freestyle Champion, speaker, coach. lewiscrathern.com
Mitu Monteiro – Wave Kitesurfing world champion F-onekites.com

## Instructor contributors

Molly Parr –South East England - Heike Bielek - Greece/Asia - Robbie Anderson – ikoint.com - Clive Marriner - South East England  - Tom, Tristan and Rupert Cawte – TheKitesurfCentre.com Camber Sands  England - Steve Sinnhuber – learntokitesurf.co.uk South England - Kevin Mattey - UK - Ben Clarke – England/South Africa - Hawaiis Doumtsios – Surf Club Keros, Limnos, Greece surfclubkeros.com Adham Ahmer –Somer bay Egypt and UK - Mowgli Leondelaplaya –Peru/Namibia/Cape Town - Adrian Fefer - South Africa/Carribean/Mexico - Wolfram Reiners – kitekahunas.com Cape town South Africa - Seb Gyde  - New Zealand, South Africa, UK.- David Furney - Ireland/New Zealand - Lou Green - UK/South Africa

## Contributing Kitesurfing legends

Ben Northover, Dan Simon, Thomas Framnes, Matteo Lombardi, Richard Branson, Selin Sohtorik, Astrid Jansen, Rob Spickett, David Giles, Gordon Jessop, Marc Haendel, Matt Bellamy, Patrick Stein-Kaempfe, Stein Van Der Weiden, Evrim Blauth, Clive Peacock, George Chandler, Caroline Morris Special thanks to **Lou Green** for all her modelling work, without Lou the photos would not have been possible. Ruth Williams for inspiration, Rupert Cawte and his relentless design work, ideas and working on a promise! Also the whole team at web-active.co.za namely Debby for being phenominal, Louise for her TRULY AMAZING artwork and Novas incredible webskilz, Clive and Helen at Artwrite for all printing and thekitesurfcentre.com for all their support, also Cabrinha kites, Ozone Kites and Core kites for their kind help and lastly but by no means least Mowgli Leondelaplaya for his relentless work on the German version of this book and for being a great friend. Thanks everyone.

This book has been written and produced to help the reader to learn to Kitesurf as fast as possible while having Kitesurfing lessons from a professionally recognised Kitesurfing instructor.

The audiobook version has been designed to be used as a refresher course for someone who has had a break from Kitesurfing and could be listened to while driving to the beach.

There are many Kitesurfing techniques and this book does not in any way claim to be the only or safest way to perform any of the following Kitesurfing activities. Kitesurfing will forever be evolving and many of the techniques explained in this book could be out of date as soon as the book is published. However at the time of writing, the techniques used have been carefully considered to be of the greatest use to the reader and to promote safe Kitesurfing.

## About the author

Tom Fuller has been teaching Kitesurfing since 2007 and kiting since 1999. His career highlights in Kitesurfing include Kiting across the English channel, running Kitesurfing camps for disabled riders, becoming a senior BKSA instructor, competing in the SA Wave Kitesurfing masters, running schools operations as head instructor in SA and Greece, becoming an instructor trainer for the IKO, producing a series of wave kitesurfing instructional movies as narrator and cowriter plus having a continual thirst and determination to be of value to as many kitesurfers as possible as well as improve his own teaching and riding. You can find Tom in the Turks and Caicos islands @bigbluecollective

Please help to improve future versions of this book! If you can see any mistakes or see any ways that this book can be improved so it can give more value to the readers then Tom would love to hear from you. Contact **tom@tomskiteboardingtips.com**

**Legal disclaimer** The information in this book is provided as a guideline for application only if approved by a certified Kitesurfing instructor for your specific equipment and ability level. The author of Learn to Kitesurf faster assumes no liability for user application of the information in this book, and any application of the information in this book is at your own risk. Kitesurfing is a dangerous sport and unfortunately it can carry the possibility of injury or death to yourself or others. Always follow manufacturer instructions of your equipment and the directions of a certified Kitesurfing instructor.

Special thanks go to the authors favorite (and the worlds most ecofriendly) Kite brand

INSPIRED BY NATURE · DRIVEN BY THE ELEMENTS

# Contents

# So you want to learn to Kitesurf? Know this...

- Yes, it's even more fun than it looks.
- Kitesurf will change your life.
- You do not need to be strong to Kitesurf.
- Almost anyone can learn to Kitesurf. From 4 years old to over 80 and beyond.
- Having lessons from a professional instructor even after you can Kitesurf will help you to  progress and have even more fun.
- People with certain disabilities can also learn and enjoy Kitesurfing at a specialist centre.

## THE MA3IC THREE

Throughout the book you will notice there is a round up at the end of each section with the three most important points.

Kitesurfing can be separated into two main sections, safety and riding.  Here are the magic three for each of them.

### Kitesurfing safety
1. Always check the wind and the suitability of your location    before you go Kitesurfing
2. Know that the most dangerous part of Kitesurfing is the launch
3. Know that the most common injury in Kitesurfing is a broken ankle from falling over in shallow water that is below your knee. Stay in water above your knee.

### How to ride
1. Build power slowly, start small and build the power up.
2. You have to stand up but keep your legs bent for your first board starts.
3. You go where your kite goes so keep it low and at the edge of the window.

# Rider Advice

Throughout the book to help inspire you to continue your Kitesurfing journey some Kitesurfing world champions, famous Kitesurfing billionaires, highly experienced Kitesurfing instructors and some true legends of Kitesurfing from all over the world were asked exclusively for this book what advise they would give to anyone learning to Kitesurf. Here's what a few of them said. The more technical advice can be found at the end of the book.

*"Don't be put off by the perceived complexity of kiting, or the difficulty and frustrations you may experience when you first start, it really is simpler than you think and one of the most liberating experiences in the world. I've never participated in a sport that has allowed me to explore the world in the way kiting has. Stick with it, the reward is well worth the effort!!"*
**David Giles - Wave Kitesurfing enthusiast Perth, Australia.**

*"Kiteboarding is my key to ultimate freedom. You can totally rock it at your own pace, go for a nice sunset cruise, ride the waves or boost as big as you can in a gnarly storm. There's something for everyone. The youngest Kiteboarder is 3 years and the oldest close to 90, so no excuses there. It took me 3/4 months to learn in 2000 but once I got the hang of*

*it, it has been smooth sailing and a lot of fun. Plus it comes with the best lifestyle possible… active, healthy and sustainable. Get involved!"* **Ruben Lenten – Red Bull King of the Air Champion, Professional Kitesurfer, early pioneer of the Megaloop and extreme riding len10.com**

*"The sky is the limit, but you´ve got to start from somewhere … so here you are: embrace your power and strength which lies in you, with a determined mind you can achieve everything. Stay calm and relaxed, always remember that your energy is given by mother earth so give love back and enjoy every moment you spend on this Kitesurfing journey on this beautiful planet, she nourishes you with beautiful sun rays, wind and waves … go and explore the world with your kite, paint some pictures while shredding the waves on a sunset session, get inspired while enjoying this amazing sport that we all love so much."* **Mowgli Leondelaplaya – International Kitesurfing instructor.**

*"Kitesurfing is not just a sport it's a way of life. It provides an amazing lifestyle, enabling you to embrace the wonderful environment in which Kitesurfing encompasses. The water, the sunshine, the sounds, smells and colours, all the sensations it offers cannot help but have an*

*amazing impact on your emotional wellbeing and physical health. For me, Kitesurfing is a tool for personal growth, a pathway to adventure, a chance to experience true happiness and an opportunity to feel the Kitesurfing love. For anyone new*

to Kitesurfing who has just finished their lessons, my advice would be to maintain your determination. The learning process can be very challenging and push you to explore your own personal limits. If you can, set aside a serious amount of time to consolidate your learning and to practice but stick with it, once you get up on the board and get your first runs in, you'll be hooked! X" **Lou Green - International Kitesurfing Instructor and Kitesurfing model**

 "*Sometimes is the smallest decisions that can change your life forever. Be aware of that before you really get into kiting...!! Kitesurfing is not a sport, it's a feeling!*" **Ellie Samoladou – Centre manager and instructor surfclubkeros.com Lemnos, Greece**

"*Progression comes quickly once you have the basics but don't get ahead of yourself, It's really important to take your time setting up and to be aware of others around you. On the water don't be afraid to try new things, there are so many things to enjoy in the sport so switch it up and find what works for you.*" **Aaron Hadlow Five times world freestyle champion and twice winner of the Red Bull King of the Air aaronhadlow.com**

 "*Don't be afraid to crash, do something wrong, or look stupid when you are learning. These things are part of any sport, and if you don't try because you are scared of how you will look, it will limit you. Just have fun and go for it!*" **Moona Whyte – KSP Kitesurfing World Champion Cabrinhakites.com**

"*When it's windy, go Kitesurfing. If the conditions are great, the washing can wait. Just go Kitesurfing*" **George Chandler – Kitesurfing entrepreneur Sandgate UK**

 "*Kitesurfing is the best sport that I have ever learned. I love how free it makes you feel as you play with the elements. No session is ever the same which is one of the reasons it's so exciting. I remember when I started; when I stood up for the first few meters I was totally hooked. My advice for when you have finished your lessons is that you must try to practice for as many hours as possible as that's when you really learn. Don't give up at the start, it might feel difficult at first but once you get it you won't regret all the effort you put in and don't forget to have fun ☺*" **Jalou Langeree – Professional Kitesurfer 2012 KSP World Champion. jaloulangeree.com naish.com**

"*Welcome to the club ☺ - stay safe and always bring your biggest smile ۝. For the ultimate Kitesurfing experience, knowledge is key! Know yourself, your strengths & your weaknesses. Know your gear. Know your mate(s). Know your spots & listen to the locals. Know the weather &*

*learn to read the ever changing conditions both on land & water. Respect mother nature & your fellow kiters* 🏄 " **Thomas Framnes - Kitesurfing Guesthouse Owner Camps bay, Cape Town South Africa sovnexperience.com**

*"There's no sport in the world that beats Kitesurfing. There's just no sport that I can think of that's so exhilarating and natural, powered only by the wind. I can get away from it all for hours on end. You can either use it as time to clear the mind completely or even time to plan great ideas. To be honest I'm not sure why anybody windsurfs anymore!"* **Richard Branson - Founder of the Virgin Group Virgin.com**

*"Great excitement will come, and so will frustration. Like many things in life, the key is to embrace them both with equal enthusiasm. Perseverance and optimism will prove to be the most valuable qualities through your journey of Kitesurfing. Never forget that the ocean is the purest form of beauty and freedom, enjoy every moment as if it is a privilege"* **Lyde Hydecroft - Team rider at RRD SA National Wave Kitesurfing champion**

*"Welcome to the fantastic sport of Kitesurfing, you are now part of a worldwide friendly community, we are like your new family, try to enjoy every step of your progression, respect the spots that you will be riding at, respect other beach users, take time to read the weather and local conditions, only go out in wind you can handle as a beginner and make sure you have the right size kite for your weight and wind strength, but above all keep smiling :) enjoy and have fun"* **Kevin Matthey - International Kitesurfing Instructor British Master's Champion 2015 livitadventures.com**

*"Take your time and enjoy each second of your Kitesurfing journey from the very beginning! Learn to love the process of learning to ride and you will love riding for ever"* **Hawaiis Doumtsios – Owner Surf Club Keros, Limnos, Greece surfclubkeros.com**

*"Be careful after your lessons as Kiteboarding will mess up your life and it will never be the same ;) So many people get hooked after their first or second lesson. My advice will be, keep doing the thing that puts the biggest smile on your face. I hope it will be Kiteboarding. If so that's awesome! It also doesn't really matter the way you ride if you are a total beginner or a pro at the end it's about what makes you stoked. So make sure you always find that magic feeling in anything you do even if it's not Kiteboarding"*

Kevin Langeree – Professional Kitesurfer, World Freestyle Champion, 2 x Red Bull King of the Air Champion kevinlangeree.com naishkites.com

**To get the most value from this book and to truly learn to Kitesurf faster here are some suggestions that will accelerate your progression...**

# Decide to Kitesurf! Sounds simple but this really is the key to

your success. If you just want to have a go to see if you like it, that's great but don't expect to progress very far, very quickly. Learning to Kitesurf takes time. Most people take around twenty hours of instruction before they feel ready to practice independently. Learning to Kitesurf is fun, right from the beginning
.

# Book lessons! With a professional school and with a

passionate instructor. This is extremely important as you want to be taught properly in a safe, comfortable and friendly environment using Kitesurfing equipment that is specifically designed for learning. A great instructor knows that their job is to help you to become independent, so you will be a safe, independent learner.

# Know what to expect!

When learning to Kitesurf there is a step by step process that you have to go through, there are no shortcuts. Anyone can learn to ride a board but if you fall off it and don't know how to get it back then you will be seriously limited as to where you can Kitesurf and you could end up in severe danger. Do your homework!

**Your Kitesurfing lessons should go something like this...**
1. Basic theory about essential safety, the wind window and how to fly a kite.
2. How to fly a trainer kite on the land.
3. How to set-up a Kitesurfing kite.
4. How to use your control bar and how to activate your main safety systems.
5. How to launch and land a Kitesurfing kite.
6. How to fly a Kitesurfing kite and how to relaunch it from the water.
7. How to body drag. Body dragging is where you use the power of the kite to pull you through the water without a board. You need to know how to body drag so you can recover your board in deep water and learn how to get yourself back to the land without your board. There are three main types of body drag: Downwind body

dragging, directional body dragging and upwind body dragging, you have to learn them all.

8.  How to self-rescue if something goes wrong at sea and how to self-land your kite.
9.  How to board start, how to ride on your board and most importantly how to come to a controlled stop.

**You may find that your lesson is done in a slightly different order, this could be due to the location or the conditions but this is most common and preferred process used by the most professional schools and instructors all around the world.**

# Buy a small power kite! Fly

it as often as you can, ideally in light winds. Successful Kitesurfing is achieved by a number of elements but the most important one is your ability to fly the kite. Flying a small power kite before you have your lessons is fun and will help you to learn to Kitesurf faster. If you have had a long break from Kitesurfing then flying a power kite will help you to remember what you have learnt. Teaching your friends and family to safely fly a power kite will also help improve your skills and its great fun for everyone.

## Buy some Kitesurfing equipment!

Get yourself some of your own gear as soon as you can after your lessons. When you commit to buying equipment, you are confirming to yourself that you are going to Kitesurf. New equipment is not only much safer but it is much easier to use plus having crispy new equipment will help inspire you to get out there and get the most value from your new gear and continue learning.

# Get some board skills!

Most people when starting their Kitesurfing lessons have never flown a kite and have never a ridden any other type of board. Don't worry as Kitesurfing is one of the easiest board sports to learn. The best practice for Kitesurfing is actually Kitesurfing but wakeboarding, snowboarding, surfing and even riding on a skateboard will all help you to progress faster. Any time that you spend riding any sort of board will help improve your balance. It will also help you to get used to the feeling of standing up on a board as well as giving you the chance to practice turning and it's a great excuse to have some pre-fun, fun. Whatever you do, just make sure you do safely.

## Use accelerated learning

Using more than one of your five senses can help you to retain more information. Read out loud anything you feel that you want to remember. Listen to the audiobook version of this book in your car while stuck in traffic, on the way to the beach or on your headphones while waiting in a queue or doing the washing. The action of putting pen to paper or even typing in your phones notes will help imprint information on your long term memory. Discus or teach anything that you learn with friends as just by speaking out loud in your own words will help you to understand and remember new information. You may even be able to help a friend who is also learning to Kitesurf or inspire someone else to get into Kitesurfing.

# Visualise!

Mental rehearsal and visualisation is used by most sports professionals. By closing your eyes and imagining yourself Kitesurfing, you can actually practice in your mind without moving a muscle. As you read this book you will notice pictures of people Kitesurfing, this is to help you visualise yourself riding on the board. There is a guided Kitesurfing visualisation in the bonus chapter at the end of this book.  Have a go, it's fun and it is proven to help your performance.

# Warm up!

before every session! Kitesurfing is not a highly physical sport unless of course you want to push it to the limits. You do not need to be strong and you do not need to be super fit to Kitesurf. Many people do not realise that when you are Kitesurfing you actually use very little energy and it can be extremely relaxing however it will help you to progress more rapidly if you have a reasonable level of fitness and flexibility to get you through the learning period. Warming up before your session will help you to get into the mood. Setting up your equipment is a warm up in itself but don't be shy to spend a few minutes jumping up and down or doing some push ups to get your blood pumping. Warming up can help prevent any annoying injuries. Remember to have a stretch after your session, as you will ache less the following day.

# Get insured!

Insurance is essential these days. Even if you practice safe Kitesurfing, accidents still happen. Here is just one of many, worst case scenarios that can happen to anyone. You have a freak equipment failure and a line snaps, you have to activate your main safety and then your final safety, your kite is blown away onto a road and causes traffic accident potentially causing millions of dollars of damage. An uninsured rider who had a serious accident with the public could even cause Kitesurfing to be banned on that beach. Get some Kitesurfing insurance.

# Keep your eyes on the prize! Budget for a little frustration
when you are in the early stages of learning. Part of the beauty of Kitesurfing is that you can only go when Mother Nature says so. Sometimes it feels like you are going backwards, everyone goes through it, so relax.

# Kitesurfing Equipment, what you need.
**Your instructor will choose the most suitable gear for your lesson but for your first sessions without an instructor you must have the right gear.**

# Recommended Kitesurfing equipment
- An inflatable Kitesurfing Kite, free from rips and tears that holds air and is the correct size according to your body weight and the wind speed.
- A working Kitesurfing pump that has the correct connection for your make of kite.
- A Kitesurfing specific bar and lines that can be used with your kite and has an effective, modern safety release leash system that attaches to your harness.
- A selection of modern kites in different sizes to choose from depending on the wind strength.
- A "twin tip" board that can be ridden in both directions.
- A bar that has a one line safety release system. This is when you activate your safety, your kite is attached to you by one line so there is no power.

# Recommended personal Kitesurfing equipment

- A Kitesurfing harness that fits correctly and has an emergency leash attached to the front or the side so it can be released quickly and easily.
- A line cutter
- A wetsuit of some description.
- A buoyancy aid or an impact vest designed for use in the water.
- A safety helmet that is designed to be used in the water.
- A cheap mobile phone in a waterproof bag that can be carried in a pocket or in your wetsuit for emergencies.
- Depending on your location a warm wetsuit, wetsuit boots, gloves, hat and sunscreen.

## Parts of a Kitesurfing kite

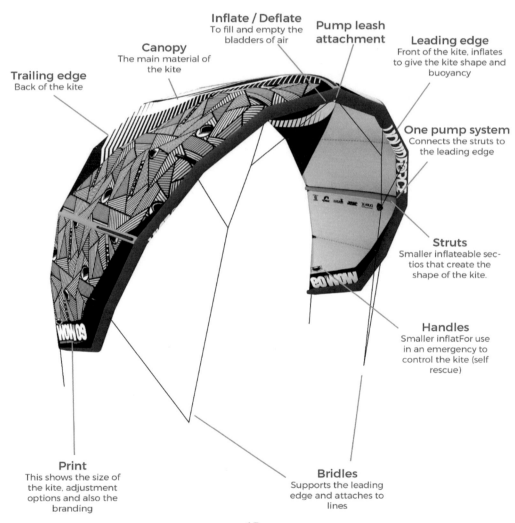

**Inflate / Deflate**
To fill and empty the bladders of air

**Pump leash attachment**

**Leading edge**
Front of the kite, inflates to give the kite shape and buoyancy

**Canopy**
The main material of the kite

**Trailing edge**
Back of the kite

**One pump system**
Connects the struts to the leading edge

**Struts**
Smaller inflateable sectios that create the shape of the kite.

**Handles**
Smaller inflatFor use in an emergency to control the kite (self rescue)

**Print**
This shows the size of the kite, adjustment options and also the branding

**Bridles**
Supports the leading edge and attaches to lines

# Parts of a Kitesurfing Bar

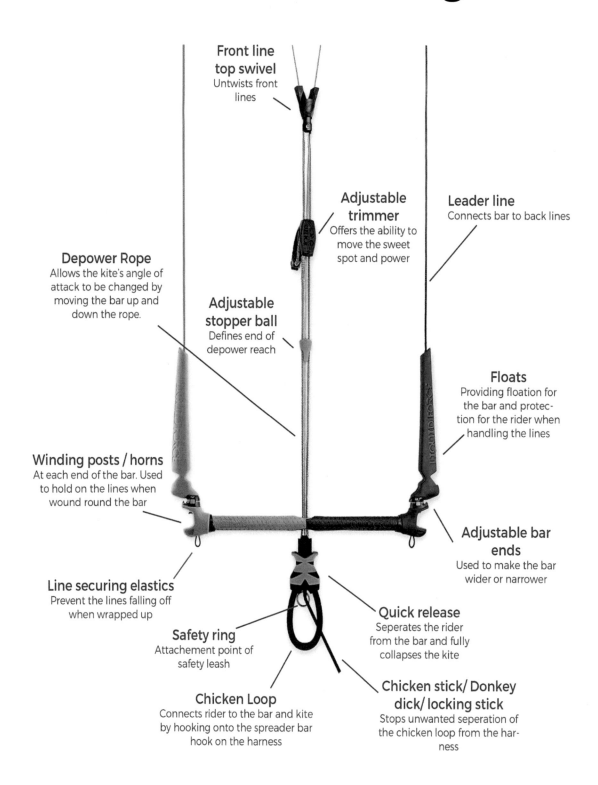

**Front line top swivel**
Untwists front lines

**Adjustable trimmer**
Offers the ability to move the sweet spot and power

**Leader line**
Connects bar to back lines

**Depower Rope**
Allows the kite's angle of attack to be changed by moving the bar up and down the rope.

**Adjustable stopper ball**
Defines end of depower reach

**Floats**
Providing floation for the bar and protection for the rider when handling the lines

**Winding posts / horns**
At each end of the bar. Used to hold on the lines when wound round the bar

**Adjustable bar ends**
Used to make the bar wider or narrower

**Line securing elastics**
Prevent the lines falling off when wrapped up

**Quick release**
Seperates the rider from the bar and fully collapses the kite

**Safety ring**
Attachement point of safety leash

**Chicken Loop**
Connects rider to the bar and kite by hooking onto the spreader bar hook on the harness

**Chicken stick/ Donkey dick/ locking stick**
Stops unwanted seperation of the chicken loop from the harness

# Before you go out check the wind and check your spot for dangers

Arguably the most important part of Kitesurfing is to decide **IF** you go Kitesurfing.

**When you arrive at your chosen Kitesurfing location, you must first check the wind and the potential dangers in the area. This is called a wind and site assessment. It takes only a few minutes and will save you a lot of time, effort, embarrassment, money and can even save your life. Make it a habit.**

A successful wind and site assessment can be the difference between having a real life nightmare or scoring the best session of your life. If you do not understand the wind or know what the potential dangers of your location are then you are risking serious injury to yourself and others. You could also cause Kitesurfing to be banned in in an area if you do not follow any local rules or if you had an accident involving a member of the public and you do not have Kitesurfing insurance.

**A wind and site assessment at the beginning of every session is one of the compulsory rituals in Kitesurfing that everyone has to do.**

**So, what is the most important part of Kitesurfing?**

# <u>The Wind!</u>

If it wasn't for the wind there would be no Kitesurfing and that would be catastrophic. Your ability to predict and assess the wind is your key to learning to Kitesurf safely and progressing as fast as possible. It doesn't matter how good you are at Kitesurfing if the wind isn't right then your session will be difficult or even impossible. The better you are at making the right decisions based on the wind, the better your Kitesurfing experience will be. It's that simple.

**You must know the answers to the following three questions.**

1.  **What is the wind strength?**
2.  **What is the wind direction?**
3.  **What is the weather forecast?**

# 1. Check the Wind Strength

**You must be sure of the actual wind speed at your location to be able to choose the right kite size.**

No matter how good you are, if you have the wrong size kite then you are going to struggle. In light wind you will use a large kite and in strong winds you will use a small kite. Choosing a kite size that is too big for your weight and the wind strength can be dangerous as you may not be able to control the power.

Choosing a kite that is too small can mean that your kite will be difficult to fly, difficult to relaunch and not provide you with enough power to pull you through the water.

*Choosing the right kite size will ensure a safer session, speed up your progression and make your whole experience much more enjoyable.*

Most Kitesurfers, sailors and wind sport enthusiasts from around the world use Knots to measure the wind strength. **10 Knots = 11.5 Mph = 18.5 KPH**

# How do you find out the strength of the wind and choose the right kite? Look at the water!

As long as the wind is coming from the sea and there are no strange tidal effects then looking at the sea is the simplest and most reliable way of knowing the wind speed so you can make the best decision on what kite size you need to use.

**When choosing your kite size you must take into consideration your body weight. Lighter riders need smaller kites and bigger riders need bigger kites.**

The following wind strength to kite size guide is based on an average rider.

1 - 8kts - The water surface is extremely calm and flat with maybe a few ripples. This is considered extreme light wind in Kitesurfing and large specialist kites are

needed ranging from 12 to even 25 meters in size. Extreme light wind is not recommended for inexperienced Kitesurfer's unless you are with an instructor in waist deep water and using specialist equipment. This is because relaunching your kite from the water in super light wind can be extremely difficult, even impossible and would mean a swim back to land or a rescue every time you crashed your kite.

9 – 14kts – The water surface is moving. You will notice many small ripples and some white caps. White caps are also known as white horses or wavelets and they are tiny waves that show a flash of white on the water surface. White caps are a good sign that there is enough wind to Kitesurf. Generally, kites sized around 11–17 meters are used. 9-14kts is a great wind speed for learning to Kitesurf. Relaunching your kite from the water is easier with a good breeze. Large kites in light winds are slower, steadier, have more consistent power and are more forgiving which means it is easier to concentrate on your body position and board control .

15 - 24kts and you will see more and more whitecaps on the water surface. You will also see small waves breaking out to sea and not just on the shore. Generally kites around 8-10 meters are used and this is a great wind speed for Kitesurfing however it is getting strong so you need to be even more respectful and cautious of the power. You can relaunch you kite more quickly with greater ease in these winds and more experienced riders are extremely happy.

25kts – 40kts and above = SUPER STRONG WIND, the water surface is full of white caps and lots of large waves are breaking out to sea. This is when Kitesurfing becomes an extreme sport. Extremely small kites are used around 4 – 7 meters. High winds like this are not recommended for learning to Kitesurf unless you are with an instructor who is experienced in teaching in high winds using specialist equipment. Relaunching in super strong wind is easy but can be much more dramatic. Small kites can also be more difficult to control because they are fast and require much more attention to fly. Crashes in strong wind are harder, equipment can get damaged more easily and serious accidents are more likely, especially when launching which is why extreme cation is recommended.

# If in doubt  don't go out!

## What other ways are there to find out the wind speed?

Looking at the state of the sea is the most reliable way to determine the speed of the wind but if you are unsure, you can use a combination of the following to help you decide what size kite to use.

## Look at Seagulls

Seagulls hover without flapping their wings when the wind is above 18 - 20kts. This means 9 meter weather to most people.

## Look at the sand on the beach.

Sand is blown across the beach when the wind is strong, usually above 25kts. For most people this means small kites.

## Look at the kites other Kitesurfers are using.

Most kite manufacturers print clearly on the side what the size of the kite is. If you see that most people are out on 6 or 7 meter kites and you only have an 11 meter then unless you are extremely heavy, you will be over powered and it will be unsafe. If you see people out on 11 and 12 meter kites and you only have a 9 then you will be underpowered unless you are extremely light. There is of course one drawback to this and that is the Kitesurfers already on the water may be on the wrong kite so use other Kitesurfers as one of many indicators as to what size kite to use.

# Talk to other Kitesurfers and ask their advice

Most Kitesurfers are extremely friendly and will help you to decide if you have the correct equipment for the wind strength and your ability.

## Use an Anemometer

If you use an electronic wind meter then make sure you take the reading from the water's edge so you get an accurate wind reading.

## Check a live wind report

Live wind reports can only be used as a guide as the reading could be incorrect. This is because the location of the wind sensor could be located in an area that is shielded from the wind or in a place where the wind is accelerated. It could even be a faulty sensor so don't always believe what the internet says.

**Note: Flags and moving trees tell you it's windy but don't tell you the wind speed.**

## Wind strength check made simple

1. Find out the strength of the wind to make the correct choice of Kite.
2. Look at the sea, look at what kites are being used, look at an accurate current wind reading, ask other Kitesurfers if you are unsure.
3. Avoid strong winds and stick to light winds while learning.

# 2. Check The Wind Direction

**You have to find out the exact wind direction before you Kitesurf to be able to control your kite and to make sure you don't get blown away from the land.**

To find out the wind direction, stand with your back to the wind, feel the wind on the side of your cheeks and listen to the noise of the wind in your ears. When you have an equal amount of noise or feeling on both sides of your face and ears then you know that the direction of the wind is blowing directly in front of you.

Firstly, for safety, you need to know what direction the wind is blowing, in relation to the land.

## Off-shore wind

**Also known as bang off-shore, straight off-shore or cross off-shore winds all blow from the land and out to the water. All off-shore wind is highly dangerous for Kitesurfing and should be avoided at all costs unless you have a rescue boat.** Off-shore wind can also be of poor quality because it has to travel over land so is more likely to become turbulent which can cause your kite to become unstable and difficult to fly making off-shore winds the worst of all the wind directions for Kitesurfing.

## Cross shore wind

**Also known as side shore wind, comes from the left or the right and blows parallel to the shore line. It can be dangerous because if something goes wrong you will not be blown back to land.** To Kitesurf in cross shore winds you need be able perform a self-rescue and a deep water pack down so you can get back to land if something went wrong.

## Straight onshore wind

**Also known as bang onshore or directly onshore wind can also be dangerous because you and your kite can be blown into the land and dangers very quickly.** Straight onshore winds can generate bigger waves on the shore which make getting in to the water tricky. Even experienced Kitesurfers can have trouble in onshore winds especially in deep water. Most Kitesurfers avoid straight onshore winds unless they have a large area of shallow water where you want walk out away from any dangers on the land.

## Cross on shore wind comes from the sea to the land at an angle from either

the left or the right. It is an easy wind direction to ride away from any dangers on the land plus if something goes wrong out to sea you will always be blown back to the land. This makes cross onshore wind the easiest and safest wind direction for Kitesurfing.

# Cross onshore wind is the easiest and safest wind direction for Kitesurfing.

### Wind Direction Check Made Simple

1. Stand with your back to the wind to find out the wind direction
2. Cross on shore winds are the easiest and safest wind directions for Kitesurfing.
3. Never Kitesurf in any off-shore winds, remember if in doubt don't go out.

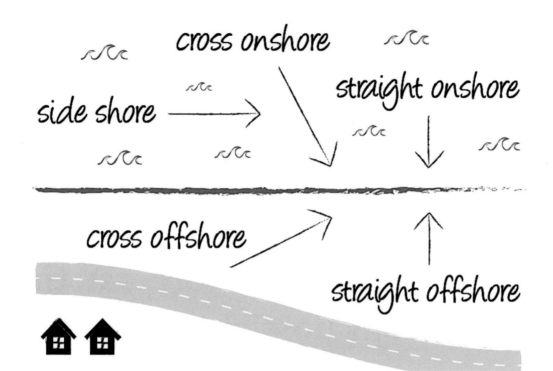

cross onshore

side shore

straight onshore

cross offshore

straight offshore

How a Kite Surfer
flys / rides into the wind.

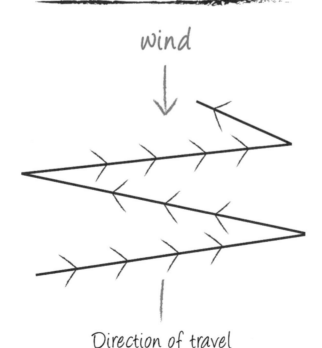

wind

Direction of travel

23

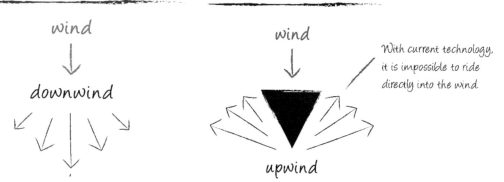

## 3. Check the weather forecast, the tides and any possible wind effects

Before you go Kitesurfing ask yourself the following questions.

- Will there be enough wind for my skill level and equipment?
- Will there be too much wind for my skill level and equipment?
- Is the wind strength going to pick up so it is too much for my skill level and equipment?
- Is the wind strength going to drop off so it is too little for my skill level and equipment?
- What will the direction of the wind be? Will it be a steady cross on shore at the beach that you intend to Kitesurf on?
- Is the wind going to be changing direction and turning into dangerous offshore winds?
- Are there any severe weather warning predicting dangerous storms, lightening of fog?
- What is the temperature of the air and water going to be?
- Will the tide effect any currents or create dangers at high tide or expose any dangers at low tide?

The best weather forecast is for stable weather with consistent wind strength and direction. The worst forecast is for wind that is stopping or changing direction as this could leave you stranded in the water having to swim or be rescued.

**High clouds or no clouds mean high pressure which usually means stable wind and stable weather. Low clouds mean low pressure so unstable and changeable wind/weather**

Use common sense but do not Kitesurf if you see lightening, the wind is dropping or changing direction, there are storm clouds or strange looking clouds or there is anything other than perfect visibility.

# Remember that a forecast is just a forecast!

A forecast is a prediction and it is only a guide as to what may happen. You cannot rely 100% on any forecast as it is just a forecast. Always check the actual wind speed and direction before you set up your kite at the water's edge.

**Wind effects that all Kitesurfers need to be aware of…….**

# The Venturi Effect

is when the wind is forced through two objects such as mountains, hills or buildings. The Venturi effect causes much higher wind speeds. This can be dangerous if you are launching near buildings because you may not be expecting higher wind speeds but this well known wind effect can also be highly beneficial as many Kitesurfing locations around the world are windy because of the Venturi effect.

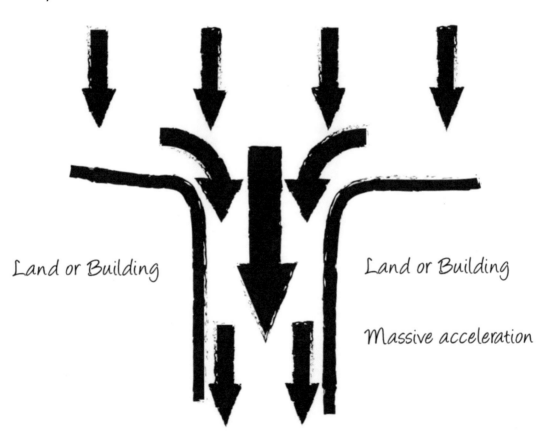

Land or Building          Land or Building

Massive acceleration

# The Sea Breeze effect

is also known as thermal wind and it is most likely to happen in cooler waters, when the sun is out.

**The sun heats the land up, the warm air rises from the land, the cooler air from the sea rushes in and causes onshore wind.**

A good sea breeze can add 20-50% more wind to a forecast and provide beautiful, consistent wind when nothing was predicted or add to existing wind and making it much stronger

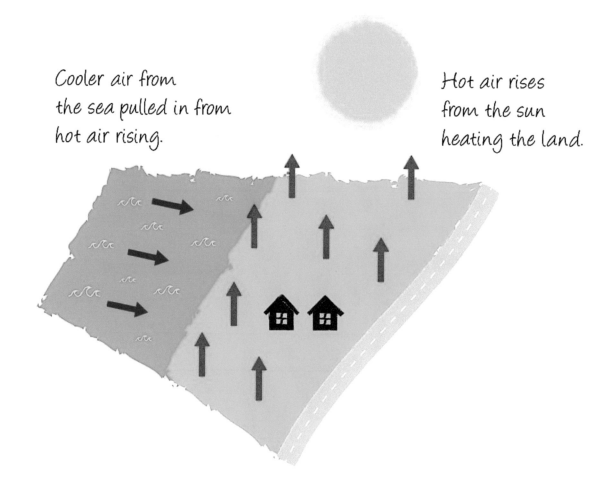

Cooler air from the sea pulled in from hot air rising.

Hot air rises from the sun heating the land.

# The Land breeze effect

is the opposite effect of a sea breeze. You need to understand it because when it happens, an onshore sea breeze can quickly turn into dangerous offshore winds.

**A land breeze is most likely to happen at the end of the day when the sun is setting or if the sun is suddenly covered by thick clouds.**

When the land cools down, the warm air stops rising and starts falling and the wind direction changes from onshore to offshore.

**If you feel the wind dropping or changing direction while you are in the sea, get back to land as soon as possible and avoid Kitesurfing after the sun goes down.**

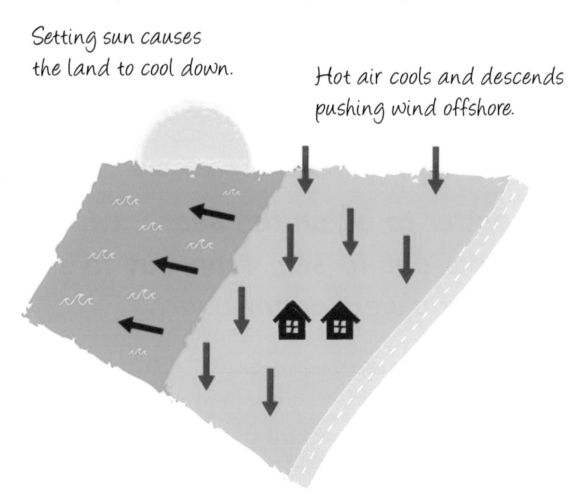

Setting sun causes the land to cool down.

Hot air cools and descends pushing wind offshore.

# A good tip regarding wind effects is to simply stay as far away as possible from any large objects.

For example, buildings, hills, cliffs, small islands and even steep slopes can all cause areas of dangerously turbulent, unpredictable and super strong wind. Wind shadows are areas of no wind that are downwind of a large object. If you fly into an area of turbulent wind or into a wind shadow from a large object, your kite is likely to fall in the water and be almost impossible to relaunch.

Other dangerous wind effects to consider are updrafts and down drafts. This is where the wind is accelerated upwards or downwards because the wind follows the land or a structure such as sand dunes or cliff. When the wind hits a slope on the beach going upwards it can increase the wind speed by up to 200%! This is why you can see birds hovering in very light wind as they use the updrafts to float.

### If you are going to Kitesurf at a new location

- Ask local Kitesurfers if there are any wind effects that you need to consider.
- Always take all of your Kitesurfing equipment with you. The weather can change quickly and you may need a bigger or a smaller kite.
- Check and confirm with locals possible tide effects that could expose hidden dangers or if there are any dangerous currents

Remember the following saying if you are unsure of any wind or location

# *"It's better to be on the beach, wishing you were out to sea, than out to sea, wishing you were on the beach"*

### Forecasts, tides and wind effects made simple

1. Always check wind, weather and tide forecasts before you go Kitesurfing.
2. Remember that a forecast is just a forecast and that you must check the actual conditions at your location.
3. Talk to local Kitesurfer's for all local wind and tide information remember if in doubt don't go out.

# Check your spot first

When you are sure that you have safe, cross onshore wind, know the wind speed, have chosen the right size kite and checked the forecast, its time to check that your location is safe for Kitesurfing.

## Some examples of dangers on the land

- Any hard objects that you could hit such as rocks, walls, seas defences, concrete, roads, cars or buildings.
- Sand or mud that you could slip over on, hard sand, sharp stones or broken glass.
- Power lines.
- Other Kitesurfers.
- Members of the public and other beach users such as fishermen, dog walkers, children playing.

## Some examples of dangers in the water

- Any hard objects that you could hit such as rocks, walls, seas defences, harbours, buoys, islands.
- Shallow water below the knee.
- Waves, currents, tidal currents and fast flowing water.

- Other water users such as swimmers, surfers, windsurfers, boats and any other water craft as well as other Kitesurfers.
- Dangerous tides such as very low tides that can reveal hidden dangers under the water surface or high tides that can cover landing areas as well as create currents or cut you off from safety.
- Sea creatures such as jelly fish or sharks.

## How can you make these dangers as safe as possible?
- First of all, make sure that you are aware of all the possible dangers at your chosen location.
- Ask other Kitesurfers, fisherman, surfers and the public. Check the internet.
- Decide if it is a safe location to Kitesurf. if it isn't then simply change location. If there are no other Kitesurfers at that location, find out why.
- **Stay DOWNWIND of any dangers. When flying a kite, you do not get pulled into the wind, you go with the wind. By placing yourself downwind of any dangers you are eliminating the chance of being pulled towards them.**
- Lastly, keep your distance, this is your greatest safety aid as distance buys you valuable time to react and activate your safety systems in an emergency.

# The absolute minimum distance between you and any dangers is <u>Two kite line lengths.</u> This is roughly between <u>50-70 meters.</u>

## The most <u>common</u> cause of accidents in Kitesurfing are the result of
- Unsafe launching of kites on the land with too much power and being too close to dangerous obstacles.
- Falling over in shallow water below the knee.

## Ask yourself - Are my skills good enough for this location?

When you are in the learning stages it should be clear to you by now that you must have plenty of space, away from any dangers. It is also easier in the beginning to practice in flat, shallow water that is above your knee and below your waist. For your first independent sessions avoid deep water, unless you have had your lessons in deep water and you are confident that you can recover your board as well as self-rescue if something went wrong. It is also wise to avoid large waves (waves are much bigger out to sea than they look from the land), busy locations or anywhere that has dangerous obstacles in the water or on the beach.

*"Safety has to come first. Every minute you spend in the water counts as valuable experience. Riding at different spots will further enhance your experience as well as improve your ability and understanding of riding in many different conditions. On top of that riding as often as you can will help you to master your kite and board control so you can enjoy yourself even more* ☺*"* **Evrim Blauth – Kitesurfing Musician**

# "The Walk of Shame"

WIND

To ride upwind means to sail into the wind or at least come back to the point at which you started. The so called "walk of shame" is where you have to walk back to where you started because you cannot Kitesurf back upwind. When you are learning to Kitesurf, you will drift No one who is new to Kitesurfing starts riding upwind immediately so you need to budget for some walking back upwind. If you have had a break from Kitesurfing and have forgot the subtle body position that riding upwind requires, there is no question that you are going to drift downwind. If you have put up a kite that is too small or the wind simply drops then you are going to drift downwind.

**This is why you must be aware of any dangers that are a long way downwind of you. Whether you are experienced or inexperienced, if there are dangers downwind of you such as swimmers, rocks, harbour walls, ship wrecks or boats then you must be aware that if you cannot ride upwind for any reason, you will be drifting downwind, towards any dangers, fast.**

If you have a lot of space at your location, you must be aware of how quickly you are drifting downwind. When you are focusing on learning or are having fun, it is easy to lose track of where you are. Drifting a long way downwind means you will have a giant walk. You could also be on your own which is also dangerous because no one will see you if you get into trouble and need help.

# General Safety Advice

- Avoid Kitesurfing alone.
- Tell someone where you are going and when you will be back.
- Study, understand and practice how to perform a self-rescue and an emergency pack down in deep water.
- Study, understand and practice how to self-land in all wind strengths and in all locations.
- Keep a simple, small emergency mobile phone in a waterproof bag which you could put in the front of your wetsuit.

## Site check made simple

1. Always take five minutes before every Kitesurfing session to check what all the potential dangers are and decide if your location is suitable for your skill level.
2. Launch and Kitesurf as far away from any potential dangers as possible, if in doubt don't go out.
3. Shallow water is the most common cause of injury in Kitesurfing, stay in water that is above your knee.

# The Wind Window

**Before you fly your kite, you need to understand the wind window**

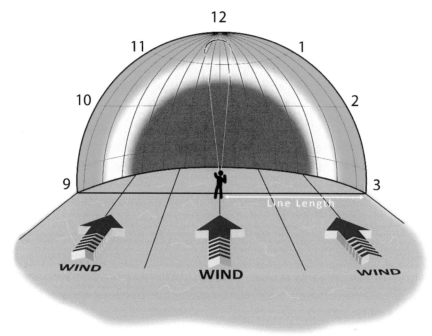

**When flying a kite you must have the wind on your back. When you are standing with the wind directly on your back, the wind window is directly in front of you.**

The wind window is shaped like a semi-circle and is numbered like a clock. With your back to the wind, if your kite is at 9 o'clock then it is directly to your left, if your kite is above your head, then it is at 12 o'clock and if your kite is directly to your right then it is at 3 o'clock. In between these positions are the same numbers of a clock and from left to right the edges of the wind window are numbered 9, 10, 11, 12, 1, 2 and 3.

**The size of the wind window is exactly the same length as your kite lines.**

**When your kite is positioned at 9, 10, 11, 12, 1, 2 and 3 it is in the no power zone. In these positions, there is the least amount of pull from your kite.**

With the wind on your back the power zone is in front of you. This is where the wind window stops being a two-dimensional semi-circle and becomes a three-dimensional quarter sphere.

**The further you fly your kite in front of you, the more power that you will feel with maximum power being directly in front of you.**

No power as the wind is blown through the kite at the top and the sides.

Wind on your back

wind ⟶

Maximum power directly infront of where the wind is caught most by your kite

33

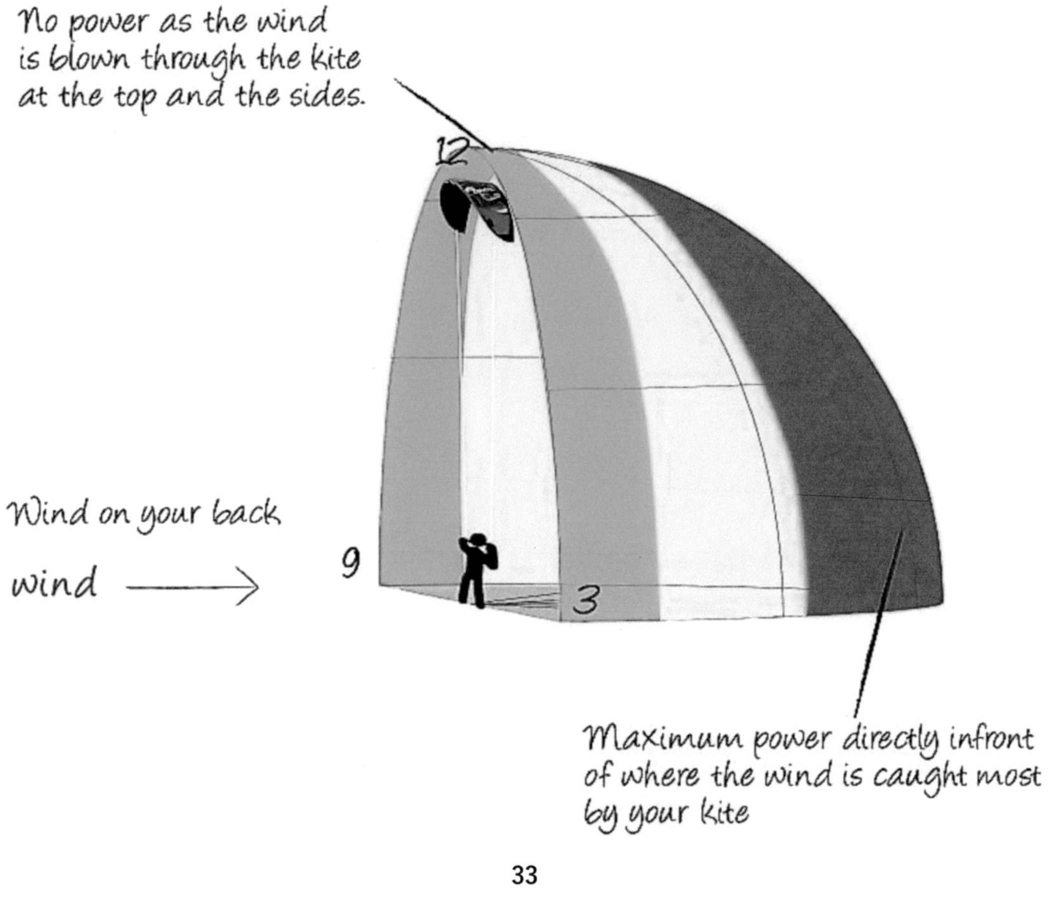

**Try this simple exercise to help you understand the wind window**
Stand with the wind directly on your back and hold both your arms out so your body is in a T shape. Your left hand is pointing to 9 and your right hand is pointing to 3. This is the extreme edges of the wind window and where there is the least power. If you keep your arms outstretched and move them as if you were going to clap directly above your head then your left hand will move through 9, 10, 11 and your right hand would move through 3, 2 and 1 and would clap at 12. These are your no power zones.

Now take your hands back out so you are standing in the T position with the wind on your back so your left hand is pointing to 9 and your right hand is pointing to 3. Keep your arms fully extended and move them together so they meet directly in front of your face as if you were clapping. When both hands meet and clap in front of your face this is pointing to the most powerful part of the power zone.

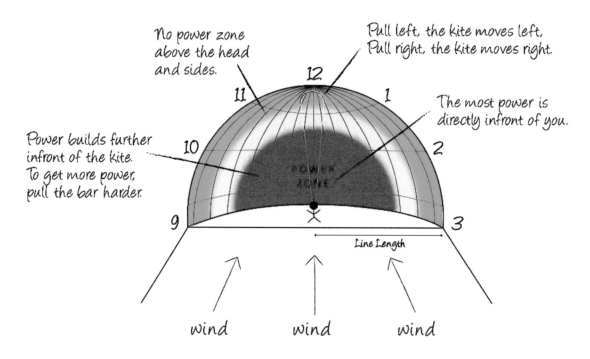

**How to fly your kite in the no power zones**
Be gentle. If you pull gently on the left side of your control bar your kite will slowly move to the left and if you pull gently on the right side of your control bar, your kite will move to your right. For example to move your kite from 9 to 10 you pull gently on your right hand and to move your kite from 2 to 1 you pull gently on your left hand. Your kite will not stay anywhere in the wind window automatically.

You have to keep in control. If you let go of your bar, your kite will simply fall down. To hold your kite in one position such as at 12, you must use small correctional movements to keep it there. For example if your kite moves slightly to the right then you must pull slightly on your left and if your kite moves slightly to your left you must pull slightly to your right.

## How to fly your kite into the power zones

Imagine that the wind is directly on your back and you have your kite positioned above your head at 12.

To get power you must move your kite into the power zone in front of you and to do this you must pull on one side of your control bar much harder. This will make your kite turn faster and it will move down and more in front of you, into the power zone.

Note: Your kite will not simply stay in the power zone, you have to keep it there. To keep your kite in the power zone you must move it up and down by pulling on either side of your bar. This is known as the....

# The Power Stroke

When you watch other Kitesurfers you will see that they keep their kite to their left or their right at 10 or 2 for most of the time.

## Kitesurfing is very simple. You go where your kite goes.

You must learn how to focus the power of your kite into one direction so you can easily ride behind it. If your kite is moving all over the wind window, the power will be inconsistent and the direction of the pull from the kite will be pulling you in many different directions making riding on a board almost impossible.

To get more consistent power in one direction, you move your kite in a figure of eight type movement on the left or the right of the power zone and this movement is called the power stroke.

**The smaller and tighter the power stroke movement is, the more focused and useable the power is.**

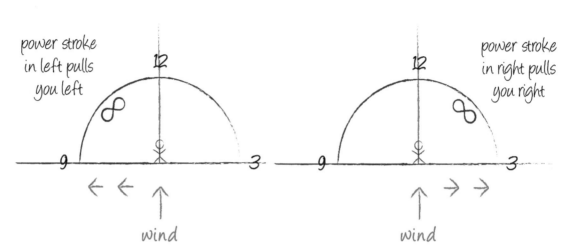

You use a power stroke to pull you through the water when learning to body drag, stand up on the board and speed up when you are on the board.

**The wind window made simple**

1. Always stand with your back to the wind.
2. The no power zone is to your extreme left and right and above your head.
3. The power zone is in front of you and the maximum power is in front of your face.

# The Kitesurfing Rights of way

Before you go out on the water it is important that you know and understand the international rights of way for Kitesurfing.

- Avoid collisions at all costs. – The most important rule.
- Give way to all other water users. – Kitesurfers have no priority.
- A Kitesurfer who has launched their kite and is entering the sea has priority over Kitesurfers who are already kitesurfing on the water – This is because flying a Kitesurfing kite on the land can be dangerous.
- If two Kitesurfers are on a collision course, the rider who has their kite on their right has the right of way - This is the same as sailing, port gives way to starboard tack.

- When passing each other, the upwind Kitesurfers kite goes up and fly's high in the sky and the downwind Kitesurfers kite goes down and fly's low in the sky
- The Kitesurfer who is upwind gives way to the Kitesurfer who is downwind – This is because the rider who is downwind has their back to the wind and cannot see the rider who is upwind.

- Give way to riders that look as if they have poor control over their equipment – Learner Kitesurfers are unpredictable.

- The Kitesurfer who is riding a wave has priority – This is because a Kitesurfer who is riding a wave cannot change their direction quickly.

# International Kitesurfing hand signals

- **Tap on the head** = Please help me launch or land my kite
- **Thumbs up** = Let go of the kite, I am ready to launch.
- **Thumbs down** = Do not let go of the kite. Abort launch.
- **Hand or both hands waving** = Emergency please help
- **Hands together in stomach centre then moved out to the sides** = Release your main safety.
- **Throat cut sign** = Abort or release your final safety

# Rules of the Road

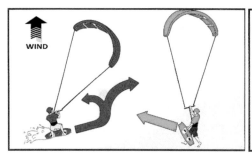

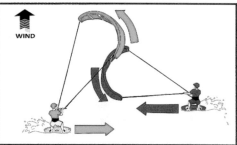

Give way to riders entering the water. Being on land with an LEI kite is more hazardous than being on water so always allow others to enter the water even if this means having to take another tack before being able to return to the beach.

When passing one another, upwind riders must put their kites up and downwind riders must put their kites down.

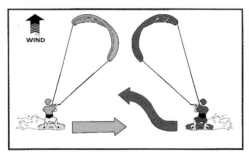

If on a colliding course give way to riders on starboard tack (generally this is right hand forward unless riding switch).

Give way to riders who are not in control of their equipment. You should give space to riders without their board or who look less in control.

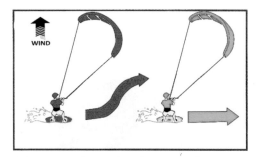

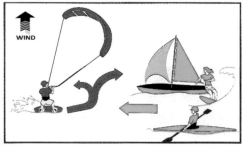

When overtaking a kiter must not obstruct or impede the kiter they are overtaking and must keep clear either to windward (upwind) or leeward (downwind) by a suitable distance.

Give way to other water users over. Remember even if it is your right of way it is your responsibility to avoid a collision at all costs and to help keep kitesurfing safe and respected as a watersport.

# Set up of your Kitesurfing kite

When you have completed your wind and site checks and you are confident that you have the skill level for your chosen location and right size kite for the conditions, it is time to set up your gear.

Walk to a clear area on the beach that is free from any obstacles and make sure that you have enough space around you to safely lay out your lines and pump up your kite without getting in any ones way or risking any damage to yourself or your equipment.

- Take your kite out of the bag first.
- Always stay upwind of your kite while handling it.
- Most modern kites now have a single inflation point. Before pumping your kite up, find your deflation valve and seal it properly. It is very important to seal this valve properly as your kite could deflate at sea if you crashed your kite.
- Connect your pumps safety hook to the kite to secure it from blowing away while you pump it up. The attachment point on your kite is located in the centre of your leading edge.
- Connect your pumps air hose to the inflation point of your kite and make sure the other end your pump hose is connected to the inflation point of your pump and not the deflation point.
- Stand with two feet on your pump.
- Let go of your kite so it is attached by the pumps safety hook.
- Start pumping. Pump slowly, there is no rush. Use full, long pump movements. Keep your arms and back straight, use the muscles in your legs to pull the pump up and your body weight to push down to make pumping your kite as easy as possible.

# How hard should you pump your kite?

The harder you pump up your kite the better it will perform.

A hard, ridged kite will turn more quickly making it feel more responsive and fly with greater stability, it will also relaunch from the water more easily. Modern kites are designed to be pumped up extremely hard.

Once you have pumped up your kite and are you are happy it has plenty of pressure

- Close the main valve. Make sure it is closed properly so it does not leak air or pop out if you crash your kite and forget to let go of your bar.
- If your kite has a single inflation point, close off all the feeder tubes that run from the main bladder to the struts. These are called strut valves and you close them by pinching them until you hear them click. This will stop your whole kite from deflating if you get a puncture in one section

- Disconnect your pump safety line.
- Hold the center of your main bladder and turn the kite over so it is in a tent like position facing down to the ground.

- Secure your kite immediately by putting on top either sand, a weighted bag or your board as a loose kite is a dangerous kite.

- Make sure your bridles are untwisted and are all the same length.

- If you are setting up in strong wind you must be even more careful when handling your kite. For example, as soon as you have flipped your kite over, do not let go of it, keep your foot on it until you have put some weight on it to secure it. Your kite can easily blow away in strong wind if you leave it unsecured just for a second.

- The safest option for securing your kite is sand bags and your board. You can fill your kite bag with stones or sand to use as a weight. When you use your board to secure your kite, place it into the wind, resting half on the main bladder and half on the ground with the fins facing to the sky so the sharp fins do not rip your kite canopy.

- Loose, dry sand can blow off your kite very quickly and make your kite unsafe. Putting stones on your kite will damage the canopy but if you have no other alternative then place stones on your kite gently.

- If you are going to leave your kite for longer than a few minutes put enough weight on your kite so it does not flap at all. A flappy kite is an unhappy kite. The flapping will damage the canopy.

## Set up of your kite made simple

1. Remember to connect your pumps safety hook to your kite
2. Pump your kite up until it is hard.
3. A lose kite is a dangerous kite, always keep your kite secured with enough weight.

# Setting up your lines

When your kite is secured properly it is time to unravel your bar and lines.
The safest way to set up is to wind your lines out directly downwind of your kite.

- Lay the ends of your lines on the ground behind your kite and slowly start unwinding. Walking slowly while you unwind your lines will help you to prevent tangles and will also make sure you do not pull your lines away from the kite.

- When you have unravelled your lines, lay your bar on the floor.
- Lay the red side of the bar on the right or lay it upside down if there is no red side.
- Separate your lines by standing in them.

- Stand with your centre lines in between your legs and have your outside lines on the outside of your body.
- Hold the four lines together in front of you and in one hand, hold your hand out as far away from your body as you can.
- Walk forward slowly and let your body untwist the lines.

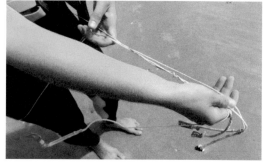

- Lay down the lines so your centre lines are clearly separated from the outside lines.
- Walk back and separate your centre lines so all four lines are clearly separated.

While you are separating your lines, check for damage or knots in the lines. If you notice a knot, untie it immediately. If you see or feel any damage to your lines, can't untie any knots or are unsure about a worn line, remember…………………

# If in doubt don't go out.

When your lines are clearly separated and free from any knots or damage, lay them out on the ground so that they are ready to connect to your kite.

## How to connect kite lines

Many accidents happen because kite lines are connected incorrectly. It is simple….

**Your outside lines connect to the outside of your kite and your centre lines connect to the inside of your kite.**

Your lines will have either a knot or a loop at each end. A knot connects to a loop.
A knot can't connect to a knot and a loop can't connect to a loop.

There are usually a number of safety systems to make sure you connect your lines correctly.

- A colour coding system. For example: Blue goes to blue, red goes to red, grey to grey and so on.
- Some kite lines are marked left and right and the attachment points on the kite will be marked the same.
- 

The outside lines will normally have a loop at the end that connects to a knot on the outside lines of the kite. The centre lines will have a  knot at the end of the lines and the loop will be on the inside connections of the kite.

All kites use the larks head knot because it is the simplest and strongest way to connect your lines together.

# How to make a Larks head knot

- Hold the line with the loop
- Push the loop through the line it is attached too.
- This makes another loop which becomes a simple slipknot.
- Put the slipknot over the knot on the line that you are connecting too.
- Pull the lines tightly so the slipknot closes and is held tightly over the knot.

The larks head knot becomes stronger under the tension of flying your kite. Make sure it is pulled tight and so it will not slip off.

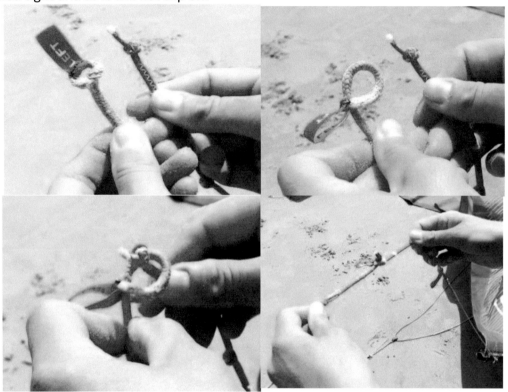

**There can be a number of different knots to connect to. Connect your outside lines to the knot that is furthest away from your kite, on some kites this may say "Low Power".** Connecting to the attachment point that is furthest away from the kite will minimise the chances of your kite flying incorrectly.

## Setting up your lines made simple

1. Walk your lines out downwind and separate them all before you connect them to your kite.
2. Connect the outside lines to the outside of the kite and the centre lines to the centre of the kite.
3. Always perform a pre-flight check to make sure your lines are connected correctly and that your main safety system works.

# How to connect yourself to your bar

- Always connect your safety leash first. Your safety leash is attached to your harness and it connects to the metal ring on your chicken loop. Check your bar system to be sure exactly where this is.
- Next connect your chicken loop to your spreader bar hook that is in front of you on your harness.
- Push the chick stick through the bottom of the spreader bar to hold your chicken loop in place.

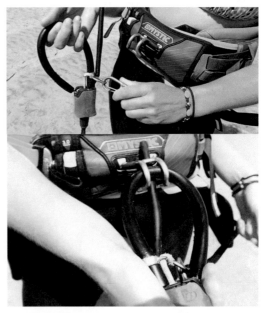

## Emergency safety systems

Before you fly any kite you must know exactly how its safety system works.

All modern Kitesurfing kites have a let go safety system. After you let go, almost all of the power will disappear and the kite will stop flying.

**Letting go is the most important safety system of all. Letting go when you crash your kite will also prevent damage to your kite.**

- If you have let go of your bar and your kite is still pulling or if you are in an emergency situation such as your kite is tangled in another kite you would activate your main safety system.
- Your main safety system is located directly in front of you and is usually clearly marked in red. The majority of safety systems are activated by pushing the red safety release away from you and then letting go of it completely as it is pulled away from you.
- Some brands have a slightly different system which is activated by a twist or even a pull. This is why you must practice activating your safety so you can quickly release yourself from the kite in an emergency situation.

Most modern kites have a simple one line safety system. This is activated when you release your main emergency safety system. After you have released your safety your kite will only be attached to you by one line and have almost no power. This is also known as a flag out system because your kite is attached to you by one point similar to a flag so cannot catch any wind and pull you.

# Practice activating your main safety with your eyes closed on the beach or at home before you fly your kite.

## Some common examples why you would activate your main safety system

- You have let go of your bar and your kite is still pulling you.
- You collide with another kite and your lines become twisted and there is no safe way to untangle.
- Your lines become tangled in an obstacle.
- You have equipment failure, such as a snapped line or your lines are twisted around your kite.
- Your kite is looping out of control and you have let go.
- You feel that you are not in control for any reason.
- You are stuck out in deep water and are unable to relaunch your kite and you need to perform a self-rescue or deep water pack down rescue.
- You have crashed your kite in waves and are unable to relaunch your kite.
- Something went wrong during launching your kite.

# Final Safety Release Systems

**You must know how your final safety system works as many are different.**

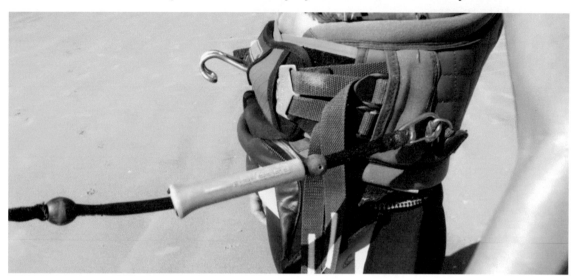

Once you have released your main safety you have the option of releasing the whole kite from your harness by using your final safety release system.

**Check that your final safety system works before every single session as part of your pre-flight check.**

It is extremely important that your safety leash is attached to a fixed point to the front or to the side of your harness on the side of your predominant hand and that the quick release is within easy reach.

## Some examples of why you would release your final safety

- You have released your main safety system and
- You are still being pulled by your kite after you released your main safety.
- You are being pulled underwater.
- You are caught in an obstacle such as a boat, another kite or similar.
- You feel that your life is in danger if you do not release all of your equipment.
- Some reasons why you do not want to release your final safety system
- In deep water, your kite is your rescue craft enabling you to perform a self-rescue or a full pack down.
- If you release your kite it can become very dangerous to other people, especially when connected to your bar and lines.

- If you do need to be rescued then you are easily located with your bright coloured kite. Without it you are a tiny dot in the ocean and very difficult to see.
- Your kite is expensive and could be damaged and lost.

**Only fully release all your equipment if your life is in danger but if you are in danger, do not hesitate to release...**

# Just do it!

*"Don't ever become complacent or overconfident. Expect the unexpected."*
Robbie Anderson - International Kitesurfing Organisation Ikoint.com

## Emergency safety systems made simple

1. Know that letting go is your first and main safety and this is the most commonly used safety system but be prepared to use your emergency safety systems at any time.
2. Know your safety systems inside out and out, know how to use them with your eyes closed and check that they are working before every session.
3. Make sure that your final safety release is attached to a fixed point to the side or the front of your harness and do not hesitate to use it if you feel that your life is in danger.

# Pre-flight check

Make sure you always perform a pre-flight check as part of your setup ritual. Do it before you launch any kite for the first time. It will save you time and energy but most importantly it could save your life.

- Once you have connected your kite lines walk back to your bar calmly.

- When you are standing back at your bar pull your lines out straight so there is a little tension. Lift one of the outside lines up to check that it is connected to the outside of your kite and that it is not crossed over with any other lines.

- Do the same to the other outside line.

- Lift up the centre lines and check that they are connected to the centre of your kite and are not twisted or crossed with any other lines.
- Check the main safety system on your bar by releasing it to make sure it works as it should do and is not damaged, worn out or clogged with sand.

# Controlling your Kite

- Your bar has to be pulled in to have control of your kite.
- Try to keep your bar flat and in line with the horizon while holding your bar, similar to the handle bars of a bicycle.
- Do not twist your bar, twisting your bar does nothing.
- Pull the right side of your bar towards you and the kite moves right, pull the left side of your bar towards you and your kite moves left.
- The less you pull the left or right of your bar towards you the slower your kite will turn.
- The harder you pull the left or the right of your bar towards you the faster your kite will turn.
- When you first fly your kite use your fingertips and be gentle.

# Power and depower

- Your control bar moves forwards and backwards. When you push your bar away, your outside lines which are also known as your steering lines become slack and the angle of your kite decreases.

- When you push your bar away, the wind passes through your kite resulting in a gradual loss of power. This is called depower.

**On most modern kites, if you push your bar as far away as you can or let go completely then you will lose all power as well as control and your kite will fall from the sky.**

When you pull your bar towards you, your steering lines have tension and the back of your kite is pulled down so it catches the wind, giving you more power.

**There are two ways to control the power of your kite**

- Pulling your bar in or pushing your bar away.
- Flying your kite in different areas of the wind window.

# Finding the sweet spot

Power is important in Kitesurfing because you need power to pull you through the water. However you do not want to have power all the time, especially when you are moving your kite around when you are launching and landing, walking on land or putting your board on in the water. You can fly your kite holding your bar in many different positions but there is an ideal  place to hold your bar to give you the most control but with the least amount of power.

This is called the sweet spot. Try to think of it as similar to a clutch biting point of a manual car transmission.

**The sweet spot can be in a different place every time you fly your kite depending on how much wind there is, how your kite is set up and even how your kite is designed.**

As a general rule the sweet spot should be when you bar is positioned somewhere around the centre of depower rope. Pulling your bar in or pushing your bar away just a few inches or centimetres can make a huge difference to how much power you feel and how responsive your kite is, so it is important that you first practice finding your sweet spot in the safety of the water.

You can deal with gusty wind by pushing the bar away as soon as you feel any unwanted power. If you have pushed your bar away and your kite is in the no power zone and you still feel power then you are overpowered and need to put up a smaller kite.

## Control of your kite made simple

1. Pull your bar in for maximum control.
2. Push your bar away to have less power and to find the sweet spot.
3. Let go to stop the power immediately.

# Preparing to launch your Kitesurfing Kite

**The most dangerous part of Kitesurfing is when you first launch your kite**

Just being aware of this fact will help you to give the launch the attention that is it deserves. Launching is safe and easy if you just follow some simple steps.

**For a safe launch with an assistant you need to**

- Have performed a pre-flight check of your setup.
- Find a launch area with at least two kite line lengths of space away from any dangers.
- Find an assistant who knows how to launch safely or is willing to learn.
- Choose the right size kite.
- Have an understanding of the wind window.
- The ability to safely control and fly a Kitesurfing kite
- Aim to have an absolute minimum of 50 meters of space away from obstacles such as rocks, people, boats and so on. The more space you have, the more time you will have to react by letting go of your bar and releasing your main safety if something does go wrong during your launch.

- Make sure you have flown a Kitesurfing kite and practiced launching on your Kitesurfing lessons with your instructor in shallow water above the knee before you attempt to launch any Kitesurfing kite.

# Visualising your launch

The first action to take in launching is to think about your launch. This is so you can visualise in your mind how the launch will take place.

Stand with your back directly to the wind exactly where you will be launching your kite. Put both your arms up to the side of you. Where your arms are pointing are the areas that you can launch your kite.

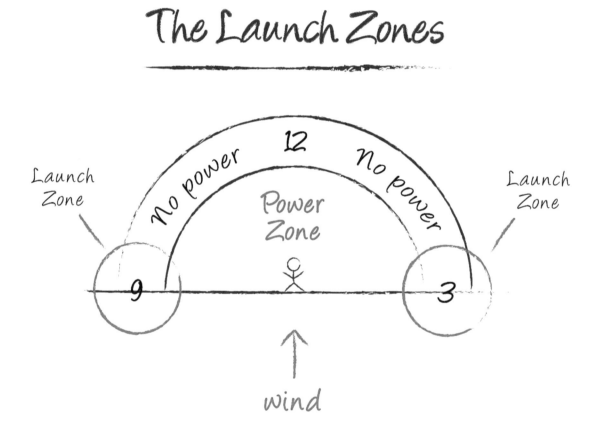

**You will always launch your kite in the no power zone at the edges of the wind window in the no power zones.**

If the sea is to your right, then launch your kite to the right. Launching your kite towards the sea means that if you have too much power, you will be pulled towards the sea and not directly towards any dangers on the land. Launching your kite towards the sea also means that you do not have to move your kite over your head while you are on the land. Flying your kite above your head while on the land is risky because you could get pulled up into the air.

**If your location has shallow water then you can launch your kite while you stand in the water with your kite towards the land. If something goes wrong and you are pulled over, your fall will be cushioned by the water but this only works if you are in flat water that is above your knee and below your waist.**

## Preparing to launch your kite made simple

1. Always perform a pre-flight check before you launch any kite by checking that the lines are connected correctly without twists and that your safety system works.
2. Make sure you launch at least two kite line lengths away from any dangers on the beach such as rocks, people or any hard objects.
3. Plan to launch your kite so you are facing the sea if it is not possible to launch your kite while standing in the water.

*"Some consider Kitesurfing an extreme sport. Either way it can be dangerous and should never be attempted by someone who has no understanding of how dangerous it can be. Seek advice from your local kite shop and most importantly seek appropriate training before changing your lifestyle forever!"* **Clive Peacock - International Kitesurfing Legend**

# Launching your Kite

- Only when you are 100% confident that you have made all the correct preparation and you are confident in your kite control is it time to launch your kite.

- You will first need to find an assistant. If possible ask another Kitesurfer to help you launch but if there are no Kitesurfers around then you need to make sure you explain clearly what they must do.

- First of all - hand your kite to your assistant in the C shape, ready to launch. Show them how to hold your kite to make it as easy and as stress free as possible.

- As you hand your kind assistant your kite, make sure that you calmly explain that all they need to do is

- Hold your kite only in the centre of the main bladder.

- Keep your kite in the C position by holding one hand in front of the other.

- Let go only when they see you give a clear thumbs up signal and only let go.

- Explain that if you need to land your kite you will tap on your head so signal that you are going to move the kite down to them where they should catch the kite by the centre of the main bladder and keep hold of it until you take it from them.
- When you are happy that your assistant knows what to do and is holding your kite correctly, it is wise to pull out your bridles so you are sure they do not wrap around the wing tips of your kite, then walk calmly back to your bar, hook your safety leash to the safety ring and connect yourself to your bar.
- Walk backwards so there is a little tension on your lines.

- Walk into the wind.

- Keep walking into the wind until your kite stops flapping. Unspin your bar so your lines are untwisted.

- Have a visual check of your safety system and that the area downwind of you is still clear of any danger

- If you are launching your kite to your right, gently hold your bar with your left hand.

- If you are launching your kite to your left, gently hold your bar with your right hand.

- Take three extra steps into the wind to be sure you have control.
- Give a clear "thumbs up" signal to your side using your free hand.

- Be prepared to let go and use your safety if something goes wrong.
- Gently move your kite up so it is around four or five meters off the ground.
- Walk calmly to the water.
- A flappy kite is an unhappy kite. It is not ready to launch if it is flapping.
- Before you give the thumbs up signal your kite should be in a perfect C shape, filled with wind and the canopy should be tight with no flapping whatsoever, if your kite is flapping then it is not ready to launch or something is wrong.

## Common launching mistakes that cause serious accidents
- A bridle has wrapped round the end of the wing tip and the kite turns into the power zone.
- The bar is pulled too hard and the kite turns into the power zone.
- The bar is not let go immediately if the kite turns into the power zone.
- The safety system is not activated quickly enough in an emergency.

## Launching your Kitesurfing kite made simple
1. Walk into the wind until your kite stops flapping at 90 degrees to the wind direction.
2. Check that a bridle hasn't twisted over the wing tip.
3. Be gentle with your bar, be prepared to let go immediately if something goes wrong and get into the water as soon as possible

# Basic flying of your Kitesurfing Kite
When you are learning to Kitesurf, it is much easier and safer, if your location has shallow water that is above your knee and below your waist. Shallow water means that you can stand up to easily practice your basic flying skills. Being able to stand up is safer because you are not constantly drifting downwind, away from where you started and towards any potential dangers.

The key to basic flying of your kite is to be gentle with your bar. Use your fingertips to start with and move your kite slowly. You do not need to be strong. If you pull your bar too hard and your kite moves through the power zone, remember to

# LET GO of your bar!

**Every kite performs slightly differently so it is a good idea to get used to your kite, the conditions and the wind window by flying your kite through the no power zone where you can practice the following exercises that will help you to progress more quickly.**

1. Practice holding your kite at 12.
2. Practice finding the best bar position otherwise known as the sweet spot.
3. Practice holding your kite at 10 and 2.
4. Practice moving your kite to the very edge of the wind window, to your extreme left or right and gently touching the kite on the surface of the water.
5. Practice moving your kite very slowly, from 9 through to 12 then to 3 and back again.
6. Practice letting go of your bar until it is natural.
7. Practice relaunching your kite from the water.
8. Practice holding your kite in one position without looking at it.
9. Practice flying your kite with one hand while standing still.

**In more detail here are the reasons why it is so important to practice each of these**

1.Holding your kite at 12 is an essential skill in Kitesurfing. The trick is to only make small adjustments of your bar. If your kite moves slightly to your left then pull very gently to your right. The less you move your bar, the less your kite will move.

2.Finding the sweet spot is also an essential skill in Kitesurfing. You have to safely control your kite on the land but with no power so you don't get pulled around. You also need to find the sweet spot so you can bring on the right amount of power to speed up and slow down when you are riding on the board. The trick is to pull your bar in just enough so you have control of the kite but you do not feel power. If you do feel power you must push the bar away a little, if you push the bar away too much then you will lose control of your kite. The sweet spot is very sensitive and moving your bar just a few centimetres can make a big difference.

3. Holding your kite at 10 or 2 is the essence of Kitesurfing. It is where you will keep your kite for the majority of your time on the water. The trick is the same as holding your kite at 12, only use small adjustments of your bar. If your kite is moving down, you need to pull on the opposite side of the bar to move it back up. If you are pulling on the opposite side of your bar and it is still moving down then you do not have the bar pulled in enough or you are not pulling on the ends of the bar, you are twisting it.

4 and 5. Practicing moving your kite from one edge of the window to the other will not only help improve your flying skills, it will also help you to see exactly where the wind window is as well as helping you to practice your turns for the future. The trick is to make sure that your kite moves over your head through 12, in the no power zone and to hold your kite with your fingertips and be extremely gentle when moving your bar.

6. Letting go of your bar is like practicing using your safety system, you cannot practice this too much. Letting go will feel unnatural at first because it is a very human instinct to hold on. If you are not quick enough to let go, you risk being pulled with great force as well as potentially damaging your kite when it crashes. The trick is simply to practice letting go so it becomes natural and automatic.

7. You have to become an expert in relaunching your kite from the water in many different positions and conditions otherwise you will spend a lot of time in the water. The trick to water relaunching is to pull on one of the steering lines line, not the bar and to be gentle and patient. Study the section on water relaunching and be sure you are confident to water relaunch before you Kitesurf near deep water.

8. Practicing holding your kite in one position without looking at it enables you to see where you are going and spot any dangers in front you as well as maintain your balance because your eyes are level with the horizon. One of the most common reasons why people who are learning to Kitesurf take longer than normal is because they are staring at their kite too much. The trick to flying your kite without looking at it, is looking at your lines in front of you. If your lines are pointing to 1 then your kite is at 1. If your lines are pointing to 11 then your kite is at 11 and so on. It is also important to know that you have to look at your kite if you are moving it aggressively.

9.Flying your kite with one hand is important to learn as there are many times when you will need to have control of your kite with only one hand.

For example: Launching your kite, walking with your kite while holding your board, putting your board on and recovering your board in deep water all require you to fly your kite with one hand.

# Flying your kite with one hand in detail

- Know that you have half the control when you are using one hand, therefor only move your kite slowly.

- Keep your bar level with the horizon and don't twist it.

- If your kite is on your right, take your right hand off the bar and use your left hand.

- If your kite is on your left take your left hand off the bar and use your right hand.

- Place your hand next to the centre lines not over them.

- Simply pulling your bar in towards you will make your kite move up.

- Simply pushing your bar away will make your kite move down

- You do not need to use any strength to fly your kite with one hand.

- Know that it is almost impossible to fly your kite on your right using your right hand.

**Basic flying of your Kitesurfing kite made simple**

1. Practice basic flying in water above your knee and below your waist so you can stand up and do not drift downwind.
2. Be gentle with the bar, you can control your kite using your fingertips.
3. Pull the bar in for control, push the bar away for less power and let go when you crash your kite.

# Relaunching your kite on the water

These are the main techniques that you will use when your kite has crashed and is in the following positions on the water.

<u>Position one.</u> **Your kite is at the edge of the window and is in a C shape on top of the water.**

This is the most common and the simplest relaunch because your kite is in the launch position.

- Unspin your bar so your lines are untwisted.
- Let go of your bar and hold on to the steering line that is attached to the wing tip that is out of the water.
- Pull gently. Seriously gently. To give you an idea of how gentle you need to be, it is possible to launch your kite with your little finger.

- As your kite comes off the water, let off tension but keep pulling gently. The lighter the wind the gentler you need to be.
- Keep pulling gently until your kite is high in the window above 11 or 1. Moving your kite high will mean you have plenty of time to get hold of your bar with your hands before it falls down.
- Make sure that your bar is the right way round which is usually red on your left.

**Position two.** **Your kite is in front of you in the power zone, facing down and is full of wind, pulling you.**

- Act quickly to stop your kite pulling you hard straight downwind as it is in the middle of the power zone.
- Unspin your bar so your lines are untwisted.
- Pull on one of the steering lines until your kite moves to the edge of the wind window and into the C shape where you can launch as normal.
- If you are in deep water and there are no dangers on the land then always choose to launch your kite on the side that will pull you closer to the land and not further out to sea.

**Position three.** **Your kite is in front of you, in the power zone but is facing you.**

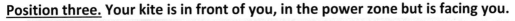

- Unspin your bar so your lines are untwisted.
- Keep pulling on one of your steering lines until your kite spins around.
- If you are pulling and your kite does not spin around, let go and pull the other steering line until your kite spins around. You may have to pull more line in than normal.
- When your kite has spun around, launch as normal.
- If your lines are twisted or crossed over, as long as red is on your left, you can fly your kite as normal to get back to the land where you can land your kite and fix your lines.

**Position four.** **Your Kite is upside down with the leading edge facing the sky.**

This happens more frequently in light wind and is known as a hot launch because it is in the middle of the power zone when it takes off and will pull you hard.

- Unspin your bar so your lines are untwisted.
- Push your bar away as far as you can.
- If your kite hasn't launched, pull hard on your centre lines.
- Prepare to be pulled though the water.
- When your kite has launched and is at least a few meters in the sky, get hold of your bar, pull the bar in as normal to get control and fly your kite as normal.
- If your kite falls over so the leading edge is facing down then carry on with a normal launch.
- Study the section in this book on hot launching

## The secrets of water relaunching
- Always leave your bar pushed out fully and pull on a steering line to launch.
- If your kite is on your right, use your left hand to pull the steering line. If your kite is on your left, use your right hand to pull the steering line. This will help because when your kite launches off the water your hands will naturally be in the right place to take hold of your bar.
- Always start by pulling gently and slowly build your pulling pressure.
- Holding above the foam floaters where the line is thicker will help give you more leverage and require less strength.

- If your kite will not relaunch on one side then try the other side. Einstein said to keep doing the same thing over and over and expecting a different result is the definition of insanity. Change to the other side.
- The launching process is the exactly the same in deep water.

## Common challenges

Your kite keeps falling back in to the water – You are pulling too hard

Your kite moves in the power zone and crashes – You are pulling too hard

You launch and you get pulled through the water– You are pulling to hard

## Relaunching your kite on the water made simple

1. Untwist your lines before you start the launch.
2. Pull gently and aim to launch at the edge of the wind window where there is the least power.
3. Launch your kite towards the land if you have the choice so you don't get pulled out to sea.

# Body dragging

All Kitesurfers are expert body draggers, even the pros. Body dragging is where you use the power of your kite to pull you through the water without your board. You have to be able to body drag to recover your board when you fall off, to get yourself back to land if the wind dropped or if you lost your board completely.

## You can body drag in the following directions:

- Directly downwind or straight downwind.
- Directional, to the left and the right but slightly downwind.
- Across the wind or very slightly into the wind.

One of the easiest ways to start body dragging is to make sure you are on your front and not on your side. This makes learning much easier as you are on top of your bar and your legs are trailing behind you which helps keep you stable.

# The secrets to body dragging

- Keep your bar pulled in for power and control of your kite.
- Keep your kite in the direction that you want to go.
- When using a power stroke, pull each end of the bar firmly and in a rhythm to make sure the power stroke is small and focused.
- To stop, move your kite to 12.

# Directional body dragging

**The most commonly used body drag is cross wind or upwind body dragging to retrieve your board after a fall.**

**With your back to the wind, to body drag to your right, use a small, focused power stroke towards 3 o'clock in the wind window. To body drag to your left, use a small focused power stroke towards 9 o'clock.**

However, there are times when you will need to body drag directly downwind.
The safest way to body drag directly down wind is to use a small power stroke at the top of the wind window between 11 and 1. You can body drag directly downwind by flying your kite directly through the power zone in light wind but it is more difficult and in stronger wind it could be dangerous. This is because you will be pulled with great force because your kite will be directly in the middle of the power zone.

# Remember to come to a controlled stop, move your kite to 12 or let go of your bar if you are out of control.

# Power Stroke Left

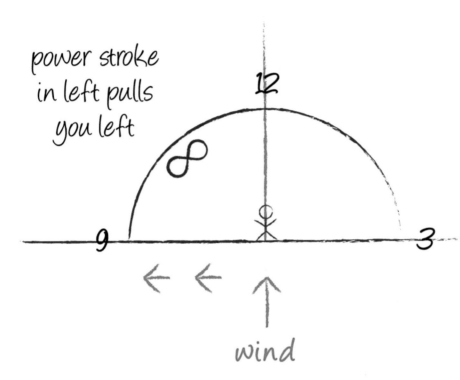

power stroke
in left pulls
you left

12

9          3

← ←   ↑

wind

WIND

# Power Stroke Right

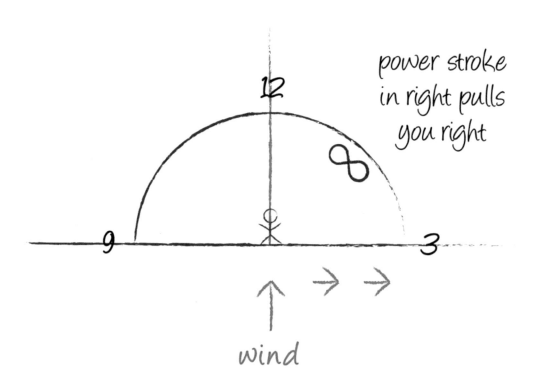

12

power stroke
in right pulls
you right

8

9                    3

wind

WIND

# Body dragging across the wind

This is also known as upwind body dragging or board recovery and it is the most commonly used of all the body drags. It is where you fly your kite at the edge of the wind window and take one hand off the bar to help you move across the wind.

## To body drag across the wind to your right
- Move your kite to 2.
- Use your left hand to control the bar and hold near the centre of the bar.
- Keep your kite at 2 by
- Pulling the bar in to move your kite higher and
- Pushing the bar away to move your kite lower.
- Take your right hand off the bar and put it in the water in front of you like superman or super women.
- Stay on your belly with your legs trailing behind and not on your side

## To body drag across the wind to your left
- Move your kite to 10.
- Use your right hand to control the bar and hold near the centre of the bar.
- Keep your kite at 10 by
- Pulling the bar in to move your kite higher and
- Pushing the bar away to move your kite lower.
- Take your left hand off the bar and put it in the water in front of you like Superman or super women.
- Stay on your belly with your legs trailing behind and not on your side.

## Body dragging made simple
1. You go where your kite goes, keep your kite low and use tight power strokes.
2. Keep your kite low in the wind window around 10 or 2
3. To stop move your kite to 12

# Board recovery

Board recovery is also known as upwind body dragging.  It is absolutely essential in Kitesurfing to be able recover your board in deep water.

Imagine you are in deep water and you have fallen off your board. Your board is now upwind of you some ten meters or even further. You cannot use your kite to pull you into the wind and you cannot swim back to your board and If you keep your kite at 12, you are drifting downwind. The secret is to remember that your board is also drifting downwind. Yes your board is coming to you so all you have to do is body drag across the wind and your board will magically appear in front of you!

# How to get your board back in detail

- Move your kite to 10 or 2, whichever side has no obstacles is best.
- Take one hand off the bar, lie on your front and body drag across the wind with one hand in front of you.
- Body drag across the wind for at least ten to fifteen meters in one direction.
- Change direction by moving your kite slowly over the top of your head, through 12 in the no power zone as this will stop you from being pulled downwind.
- Change hands when your kite is just past 12 towards your new direction.
- Body drag for at least ten to fifteen meters in the opposite direction.
- Continue body dragging left and right until you recover your board.

## Upwind Body Drag

wind

your board is being blown downwind to you

your board is coming to you

you can NOT body drag directly upwind so don't even try

Body drag with one hand to your left then to your right across the wind. Keep your kite low at 10 or 2 When you change direction move your kite over your head through 12 in the slow power section to hold your ground.

you may have to travel 3 or more times across the wind until you get back to your board

with the kite at 12 or high in the sky you are being blown downwind

# Common mistakes with board recovery

Getting dragged further away from your board is usually the result of

- Not having your kite low enough in the window – Your kite must be at 10 or 2 or a little lower.
- Crashing your kite too often – Pull your bar in to get control and to keep your kite in the air.
- Not traveling far enough away from the board – You must travel at least ten to fifteen meters in each direction before changing direction.
- Trying too hard to get back to the board by being on your side – Stay on your front and relax, know that your board is coming to you as long as you go across the wind.
- Not doing enough passes across the wind – If you are a long way from your board then you could need to make five or more passes before you can get your board.

## Losing sight of your board is usually the result of

- having a white or blue board – Get a bright colourful board.
- Not checking where your board is – Look over your shoulder or pull your bar in at 12 when changing direction to lift you out of the water to help you spot your board.
- Waves or current taking your board downwind of you – Always check downwind of you as well as upwind of you if you can't see your board.

## Crashing your kite during body dragging is usually the result of

- Not pulling the bar in enough.
- Holding the wrong side of your bar, remember that red always goes on your left.
- Holding the bar at the end and not nearer the depower rope.

## Board recovery made simple

1. If your kite is on your left, fly your kite with your right hand, If your kite is on your right, fly your kite with your left hand, pull your bar in to move your kite up and push away for it to move down, aim to keep your kite low at 10 or 2
2. Stay more on your front and not so much on your side
3. Change direction slowly and move your kite over your head and through 12 using small gentle movements of your bar

# Body dragging with your board

If you are unable to ride your board when you recover it due to your board being broken in some way such as a strap that has come undone or if the wind drops so much there is not enough to stand up, then you need to be able to body drag back to the land while holding your board.

**Body dragging with your board is the same as body dragging across the wind.**

- With your free hand, hold the handle of your board and hold your board out in front of you with the front of the board slightly out of the water.
- Keep your kite low, either at 10 or 2.
- Point your board towards your kite

# Board start preparations

If you are having troubles board starting or you want to speed up the learning process, take some time to prepare before your session by watching some Kitesurfing movies or watching other Kitesurfers. This will help you to understand the process and to visualise yourself riding the board.

One of the best exercises to practice before you board start is balance body dragging. Balance body dragging will help you to learn how to keep your body pointing downwind, keeping the wind directly on your back and holding your kite at 12, all at the same time which are all essential skills for successful board starts.

### How to balance body drag
- Start with your kite at 12.
- Put your hands in the centre of the bar but either side of the depower rope.
- Lay back in the water and put your feet up and keep them together so they are pointing directly downwind.
- If you spin to your right, take your left hand off the bar, paddle and turn your body so your feet continue to point downwind.
- If you spin to your left, take your right hand off the bar, paddle and turn your body so your feet continue to point downwind.

- If you are pointing directly downwind then relax, don't do anything and keep both hands on the bar.
- Use your hands to steady you, not your feet.

**The secret of the exercise is to keep your kite at 12. To do this most effectively, keep your hands in the centre on the bar. This gives your bar less leverage and helps keep your kite at 12, even if you pull accidently on your bar while paddling with your other hand.**

WIND

When you can balance body drag comfortably your board starts will be much easier.

## What you need to know before you attempt a board start

- Board start practice requires much more space than the minimum two kite line lengths of 50 – 70 meters as potentially, you will be traveling much further.
- Your first board starts are much easier and safer if you are in water that is above your knee and below your waist.
- Never attempt a board start or ride in water that is below your knee.
- You must have the right size kite for the wind conditions. Not enough power
- will make a board start much more difficult or even impossible. Too much power will be extremely difficult to control, will pull you downwind much more quickly and can be dangerous.
- Aim to practice in light winds with a large kite if possible. Large kites are slower and have more consistent power. High winds can be dangerous and small kites are very fast which can be difficult to control. If you have to use a small kite then hold your bar nearer the centre to slow it down.
- Adjust your board straps to be loose when you are learning. This will make it easier to get the board on your feet. Foot straps do not have to be tight in the beginning.
- You must have the wind directly on your back before you board start.
- Practice first on the side you feel will be your strongest side so you have the best chance of standing up.
- To learn faster, build the power gradually so you are not crashing your kite and falling off your board after every attempt. Be cautious to start with.
- Your kite does not pull you out of the water. You must learn forwards, extend your legs and stand up on your board. Similar to standing up from a chair.

- To come to a controlled stop, move your kite to 12, push your bar away and sit back in the water. Not knowing how to stop in a controlled way is similar to driving a car without any brakes.
- To stop immediately, if you are pulled out of the water or are out of control in any way, let go of your bar, if you are still being pulled do not hesitate to activate your main safety system.
- You must reset and start from the beginning of the board start process after every attempt.

## Board start preparations made simple

1. Practice balance body dragging before your board starts.
2. You must have the wind directly on your back before you start.
3. To stop in a controlled manor, bring your kite to 12 or simply let go in an emergency.

# The Board Start

Your first attempts to put your board on your feet and stand up, may seem impossible and that there is a lot to think about. The truth is, there is a lot to think about. Don't worry, try to relax and enjoy the learning process. After around twenty or so board starts, much of what you have to think about will become unconscious and everything becomes much easier.

## Putting your board on the easy way

**Before you ride the board, you first have to put it on your feet. If you put your board on in the same way every time, it will become a habit that you do not have to think about. One of the easiest ways to put your board on is as follows:**

- Stand in the water with the wind directly on your back.

- Move your kite slightly past 12 nearer 11.

- Put your right hand near the centre of your bar just

next to the depower rope, pull it in so it is in the sweet spot where you have a little control but no power.

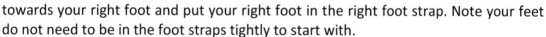

- Take your left hand off your bar.

- Hold on to the handle in the centre of your board and hold your board on your left with your left hand out to your left side.

- Sit back in the water and take both feet off the ground.

- Resist pulling on your bar while you put your board on so your kite stays at 12.

- As soon as your feet are off the ground, put your board on as quickly as possible to minimise spinning around and unwanted kite movement.

- To put your board on as quickly as possible, lift up your right foot, move your board towards your right foot and put your right foot in the right foot strap. Note your feet do not need to be in the foot straps tightly to start with.

- After your right foot is loosely in the foot strap, take your hand off the board handle and put your left foot in the left foot strap. You can hold the back of your board to help you to put your left foot in your left foot strap.

- You must put your board on. It will not magically float onto your feet. Try to keep your board in front of you as much as possible.

- Keep your kite at 12 while putting your board on by using very gentle movements of your bar.

- Remember to help stop you spinning around and keep the wind on your back, take a hand off your bar and paddle. If you spin to your left, paddle with your right hand and if you spin to your right, paddle with your left hand.

- When you get your board and with the wind on your back, keep both legs bent and Relax!

- Don't rush. Stay as you are for now. Get used to being in this position.

## Putting your board on made simple
1. Put your board on in the same way every time regardless of what direction you will be riding in so it becomes an easy habit.
2. Hold your board by the handle and put your board on, it will not magically float onto your feet.
3. If you hold your kite with your right hand, hold your board handle with your left hand and put your right foot in first.

*"Compose yourself, do one thing, compose yourself then move on to the next. Keep your kite at 12, Compose, put your board on your feet, compose, square up with your back to the wind, compose, board start. A formula one driver doesn't do everything at 200mph just because his car does. He relaxes and then he moves."* **Clive Mariner - International Kitesurfing Instructor**

*"Go Kitesurfing on a regular basis. At the time of learning, it's essential to keep everything familiar as it's easy to forget things. Long periods of time between your next sessions will make it harder to progress. Setting up will become easier and second nature in the end! Don't be afraid to not go out if the conditions are not ideal."* **Lewis Crathern – Pier jumper, British Champion, coach. lewiscrathern.com**

# *"Remember to let go of the bar if it all goes wrong!"*
**Rupert Cawte –Owner TheKitesurfCentre.co.uk Camber sands UK**

# Board start theory

The plan now is to build the power gradually. This will help to slow everything down. When board starting remember that you want to be standing up and riding off slowly. Slowing everything down will make your board starts easier and more fun.

**It important that you understand that the more you dive your kite in front of you, into the power zone, the more power and the more speed and pull that you will experience. The less you dive your kite and the further to your sides that you move your kite, the less power and pull you will feel.**

To ride to your left, you must move and fly your kite on your left and to ride to your right you move and fly your kite on your right. Kitesurfing is actually very simple. Next it is important for you to understand that you are going to move your kite into the power zone and then back out of the power zone. If you keep pulling on one side of your bar your kite will crash in the water.

Let's say you are going to ride to your left, you will pull on the left side of your bar to initiate the board start, then at the same time as you stand up you will pull on the right side of your bar to move your kite out of the power and to keep your kite in the air.

**If you pull on the left side of your bar too gently you will not have enough power to stand up. If you pull too hard you will go flying forwards, you would have to let go of your bar, crash your kite and fall off your board. While flying forwards in a spectacular superman position is all part of the learning process and is actually quite good fun, you can minimise it and save your energy, if you simply build the power slowly.**

To build the power slowly you must be cautious and move your kite into the power zone little by little. Put simply, this means that for your first board starts, you pull very gently on the side of your bar, in the direction that you want to board start in. If you do not have enough power to stand up the first time, don't worry, just start from the beginning.

## Board start theory made simple

1. Each time you board start you must be positioned with your back to the wind.
2. Your kite does not pull you up out of the water. You learn forwards, extend your legs, and stand up slowly.
3. Be cautious to start, build the power slowly and aim to get to the level where each attempt does not end in a crash.

# Standing up on the board

**In the most basic format possible this is how you board start to your left....**

- The wind must be directly on your back.
- Move your kite to 1.
- Pull your bar in.
- Bend your legs and keep them bent.

- Pull the left side of your bar firmly so your kite moves to the left from 1 to 10.
- As you feel the board being pushed towards you, lean forwards, extend your legs and stand up.

- As you stand up pull firmly on the right side of your bar.
- When you stand up, do not fully extend your legs, lean backwards and put more pressure in your heels.

**In more detail, this is how you board start to your right**

- Before you start, you must have the wind on your back, check the area in front of you is clear.
- Face slightly to your right, keep your knees bent and put pressure in your heels.
- Slowly move your kite to 11.
- Pull your bar in enough so you feel a little pull and keep your bar pulled in.

- Pull firmly on the right side of your bar to move your kite into the power zone from 11 to 2.
- As you feel your board being pushed towards you, extend your legs, lean forwards and stand up.
- As you stand up, pull firmly on the right side of your bar to keep your kite in the air and to move your kite out of the power zone.
- Do not fully extend your legs, stay low, lean back and keep your body weight over your heels so your board is not flat on the water but at a slight angle.

**If you did not have enough power to stand up properly...**

- Take your kite back to 12.
- Make sure the wind is directly on your back, take a hand off the bar and use it to paddle yourself back into position so the wind is on your back.

- Start the board start process again but this time, to get more power, pull your bar in slightly more and keep pulling for slightly longer so your kite moves slightly faster and slightly lower into the power zone.
- Have patience and continue building the power gradually until you stand up for a few meters

# Board start summary

Kite position - Start with your kite positioned at 11 or 1 in the wind window then move it down in the direction you want to go. Start from 12 if you have lots of wind or lots of power. Remember that you must move your kite low in the window so you are pulled across the water in the direction you want to go.

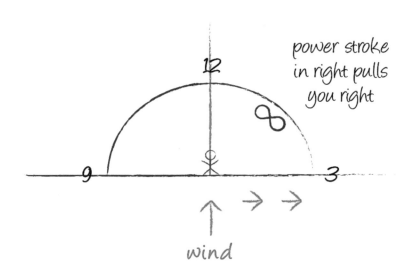

Board position – Your board is roughly at a 45 degree angle in the water, fins pointing across the wind but more towards the pull of the kite to start with.

Body position – You know by now that you must be facing directly downwind with the wind on your back and have both your legs bent throughout the whole board start. Keep your weight over your heels and lean back

Bar position – If you have a lot of power in your kite then it is advisable to have your bar pulled in around half way but you need a good amount of power to get you up on your board so don't be afraid to pull your bar in and keep it pulled in. If you push your bar away you lose power very quickly however consistent power is key to making your board start as slow and as easy as possible.

If you board start with your bar in a different position every time, then your progression will be slower and more difficult. There are two ways to control the power

from your kite. Firstly, how much you pull the bar in and secondly how far you move your kite into the different areas of the power zone.

When you board start, if you pull your bar in all the way and keep it there while you board start, you will have maximum responsiveness and maximum power. This means you will have to move your kite much less. Less movement of your kite means it will be easier to keep your kite in the sky and the less you have to concentrate on flying your kite leaving you to focus on standing up and riding.

Board starting with your bar pulled in and keeping it pulled in throughout every board start can also help if you are struggling with your balance. This is because you can push your bar away to help shift your body weight if you lean to far forwards. Pushing your bar away will also slow you down.

# If you are rising up out of the water even just for a few seconds Congratulations, you are officially now Kitesurfing. Just.

## The board start made simple

1. Wind on your back, check in front of you that it is safe to board start.
2. Kite to 1 or 11, pull your bar in.
3. Dive your kite to the direction you want to go, lean forwards, extend your legs and stand up but do not fully extend your legs.

# How to ride further and control your speed

You are now standing up on your board but only for a few meters, it's time to get in control of the power, your speed, your kite and your body position and ride further and further.

If you are slowing down and beginning to sink into the water, you are running out of power and if you are going too fast and are out of control, you need to take action.

To ride further and to control your speed follow these sequences

**To get more power, to stop sinking and to speed up, take the following actions immediately and in the following order.**

1. Pull your bar in all the way.
2. Move your kite aggressively back into the power by pulling hard on your opposite hand.
3. Come off your edge by leaning forwards and turn your front hip towards the kite. This will point your board towards the pull of the kite and you will require less power to keep riding.

**If you are going too fast and have too much power, to slow down, take the following actions immediately and in the following order.**

1. Push the bar away from your body and keep your bar pushed out until you slow down.
2. Keep or move your kite lower in the wind window to at least 10 or 2 so you can lean back.
3. Apply more pressure in your heels so you can edge harder and turn your head away from your kite and over your shoulder.

# Board starting on your less natural side

To get back to where you started and to ride upwind, you have to be able to ride in both directions, to your left and to your right. Naturally one side will feel easier than the other. Don't get frustrated too easily when board starting on your less natural side as everyone has a side that feels more difficult at first. The trick is to practice on both sides while you are learning.

**The benefits of training board starts in both directions**
- Training your less natural side will make your stronger side even stronger.
- You will have less walking back up wind.

**If you struggle on your less natural side then it is most likely that you are**

- Pointing your board too far away from your kite and not pointing the board towards the direction of the pull from your kite, enough. Otherwise known as pointing your board too far upwind.
- Not moving your kite into the power zone or pulling your bar in to bring on enough power.
- Keeping your legs too stiff and straight and expecting the kite to pull you up out of the water.

**Solutions include**
- More practice on your less natural side.
- Point your board across the wind or more downwind.
- Bring on a little more power.
- Bend your legs even more and loosen up.

# Common board start challenges

At some point all Kitesurfers have had to deal with at least one of the following challenges. Most riders have had to deal with all of them, it's part of learning to Kitesurf.

## The Challenge
You keep falling over the front of your board.

- This is because you are bringing on too much power or you are extending your legs fully.

## The Solutions

- Be even more cautious with the power. Dive your kite down in to the power less by pulling less on your front hand. Start with your kite no further back in the wind window than 1 or 11.
- Keep your legs bent all the time, lean back and stay low.

## The Challenge

You are finding it difficult to stand up.

- This is because you have not got enough power, are not facing downwind or because you are not pushing back against your board by leaning forwards and extending your legs as you are pulled by your power stroke.

## The Solutions

- To get more power, pull your bar in, pull it all the way to your stopper and hold it on maximum if you have too.

- Pull even harder on the side of the bar in the direction that you are board starting in. This will move your kite more into the power zone in front of you.

- Make sure you start the board start with your kite back to 1 or 11 in the opposite direction that you are intending to board start in. You need more power to initially stand up and to get going.

- Make sure that you have the wind on your back and that you are facing downwind so you are pulled from your front and not to your side.

- Remember your kite doesn't pull you out of the water, you have to stand up by pushing against your board as you dive your kite into the power when you feel the pull.

## The Challenge
You stand up then skid over the water

This is because you have not pointed your board towards the pull of your kite and have probably bought on a bit too much power.

## The Solutions

- Turn your front hip so your board is pointing more towards the direction you are being pulled in. Otherwise known as more downwind.

- Bring on less power. This will make your board start slower and will give you more time to react.

## The Challenge
You keep crashing your kite.

This is usually because you are not concentrating on your kite, have not pulled the bar in enough to gain control or are flying your kite too close to the water.

## The Solutions

- Keep your kite in the sky. Focus on your kite. Your kite is everything. It is the most important bit of equipment in Kitesurfing. It can get you back to land. It can turn into a sailing boat and rescue you. Your kite pulls you along on your board so don't give up on it and only let go of your bar in an emergency, if you really have too.

- Pull your bar in to get control

- If your kite is falling to your left, pull the right side of your bar and if it falls to your right pull on the left side of your bar.

- Remember that you must pull on the opposite side of your bar when you first stand up during your board starts.

- Move your kite less. If you need more power, pull your bar in. You don't have to move your kite so much to get power if your bar is pulled in

- Imagine you are in a kite flying competition and if you keep your kite in the air, you win a million dollars, unless you are fabulously wealthy you would keep your kite in the air

## The Challenge
You keep sinking when trying to ride away.

You are running out of power. Make sure you have the right size kite. Keep the power on.

## The Solutions
- Pull in your bar.

- Move your kite quickly, right back into the power zone.
- Lean more forwards, turn your front hip towards the kite.
- Pump up a bigger kite or get a bigger board.

## The Challenge
You spin around when you put your board on.

This is usually because you are doing nothing to stop yourself from spinning around.

## The Solutions
- Practice balance body dragging
- See section on balance body dragging
- Paddle with your hands to steady yourself. If you spin to your left, take your right hand off and paddle, if you spin to your right, take your left hand off and paddle.
- Stop staring at your kite all the time and look in front of you. Don't be a kite Zombie. You can look at the lines to see where your kite is in the sky.
- Keep both your legs bent the same amount.

## The Challenge
You are having trouble putting your board on Don't worry, it usually only happens when you are first learning.

## The Solutions
- Loosen your foot straps so they are as big as they can go.
- Practice putting your board on in the water without your kite.
- Keep to the same ritual of putting your board on every time and then it becomes automatic.

- Use your right hand to hold the kite, your left hand to hold the board, sit back in the water and put your right foot in first.
- Resist pulling on your bar while you put your board on.
- When you are ready to put your board on, put it on as quickly as possible.
- If you are really struggling because of body limitations, if it is safe to do so you could land your kite on the water and let go of the bar while you put your board on.

# Riding upwind

The day that you come back to the same place that you started from and no longer have to walk is a very satisfying day in Kitesurfing. As you progress further, you will be able to travel anywhere you want across the water and your whole life will improve.

## The secrets of riding upwind are
- Having enough power in your kite.
- Know that when you board start you must first bear off downwind, towards the pull of your kite and gain a little speed before you can attempt to ride into the wind.
- To be able to ride consistently in both directions.
- To be able to change direction in a controlled way.
- To be able to control your speed and ride slowly.
- To have the right body and kite position.
- Riding far enough in each direction.
- Putting more pressure in your back foot.
- Looking upwind and turning your head and shoulders to face upwind.

**You have to have plenty of power in your kite to be able to edge into the wind. Every time you send your kite back into the window to look for more power by power stroking, you will be pulled downwind.**

You want to have enough power so you can keep your kite low in the wind window at either 10 or 2 and just pull in your bar to speed up or slow down.

**Consistency is everything when riding upwind. Less movement of your kite and only small adjustments of your body are required as the changes in your kite and body position are subtle.**

With your kite low in the window at 10 or 2 then you can lean back further, turn your head and shoulders away from the kite and put more pressure in your heels and back foot. This will slow you down as you are resisting against the pull of your kite by turning away from the kite and in to the wind. The slower you can go the further you will travel upwind. The ideal speed is to be moving fast enough to be able to stay up on top of the water without sinking.

**You must consistently travel around 100 meters in each direction, to successfully ride upwind.**

Turning is also crucial to stay upwind. To begin with, it is easier to practice coming to a controlled stop than to link your turns. Coming to a controlled stop is the perfect practice for linked turns and it will give you the best chance of staying upwind as well as having more time to practice rather than continually walking back upwind.

## Come to a stop slowly by moving your kite to 12, slowly sit back down in the water and then simply board start in the opposite direction if you haven't mastered your linked turns yet.

Your body position is also important. Both legs should still be bent but your front leg can now be slightly straighter. You can apply more pressure on your back foot as you are now redirecting the pull of your kite. Your head and shoulders can be turned away from your kite and facing away more into the wind.

Pick a point on the horizon that is further upwind than you think you can go and turn your head to face it. Doing this will turn your shoulders which will then turn the rest of your body into the right position. Remember the saying "Aim for the starts and you might just get to the moon".

**Taking one hand off your bar while riding can help you to get the correct body position. Take your right hand off your bar if you are riding to your right and take your left hand off your bar if you are riding to your right.**

In extreme light wind or if you are underpowered, lean forwards slightly so you have less of your heel edge in the water and turn your body so your board is pointing upwind. This means that you will be using your fins more to get upwind rather than the edge of your board. Coming off your edge and leaning slightly forwards means that you will have more surface area of your board on top of the water giving less resistance, more float and use less power from your kite.

Lastly you should know that your board can make a big difference to your upwind performance. Flexible boards and small boards can suck a lot of power from your kite. The larger and stiffer your board, the easier your progression will be.

### Riding upwind made simple
- Make sure you have plenty of power so you can keep your kite low and hold it at 10 or 2 without moving it.
- Ride slowly, control your speed, change direction slowly by moving your kite slowly through 12 to the new direction.
- Pick a point a long way upwind, turn your head towards it, lean back and straighten your front leg slightly.

# Walking with your kite on the land

Every Kitesurfer has to be able to walk on the land while holding their board with one hand, usually it's just to get to the water but even experienced and pro Kitesurfers have to walk back up wind if the weather changes and the wind drops.Walking on the land while holding your kite can be risky as well

as taking time and energy so here's how to minimise your time walking on the beach.

- Set your kite up as near to the water as you can.
- Practice coming to a controlled stop and practice riding in both directions to minimise how far you have to walk back upwind while learning.
- Put up the right sized kite, this will mean you have plenty of power so you have every chance of staying upwind.
- Be aware of your location and how far you are away from where you started

**If you are not staying upwind and are clearly drifting downwind each time you go out and come back again. Stop. Cut your losses. Start walking back before you have a huge walk back upwind that could be dangerous.**

**If you have to walk back upwind with your kite**

- Make sure you have previously practiced one handed flying in the sea and are confident flying your kite with one hand.
- Remember the golden rule of one handed flying that if your kite in on your right take your right hand off your bar and if your kite is on your left, take your left hand off your bar.
- When flying with one hand know that pulling your bar in helps your kite move up and pushing your bar away will make your kite move down.
- Hold your board by its handle with your free hand.
- Fly your kite towards the water and stay as far away from obstacles and dangers on the land as much as possible.

WIND →

- Don't be afraid to let go at any time and remember that your kite is much more important than your board.

- If you cannot walk back upwind easily, land your kite to an assistant or self-land by activating your main safety system.

# Self Landing

When learning to board start and building up longer and longer runs on your board, no matter how careful you are regarding your distance, there is a good chance than you will drift downwind and be in the situation where no one is around to help you land your kite. This is why it is essential to know how to land your kite yourself.

## Before you self-land
- Make sure you have at least two kite line lengths of clear space downwind of you that is without dangerous obstacles or anything that could damage your kite.
- Self-landing on soft sand or shallow water is ideal but don't be put off by small stones.
- Know what safety system your bar has. Most modern kites have a one line, flag out system which gives 100% depower when the safety is activated and makes self-landing possible in all wind strengths.

There are several ways to self-land, some techniques require a fixed object to secure your chicken loop too such as a post or a tree and other techniques will only work in light winds. **The following technique can be used in all conditions, without a fixed object and on almost any beach.**

- Move your kite to the edge of the wind window in the no power zone at either 9 or 3, ideally away from the land.

- Let go of your bar and immediately activate your main safety system.

You are now attached to your kite by one line, your bar has moved towards your kite, and your kite should not be pulling you and will fall to the ground.

Pull yourself towards your kite by pulling yourself up the safety line using the "hand over hand, thumbs up" technique. This means you hold your safety line with the palms of your hands facing to the ground while holding your thumbs out.

Walk slowly towards your kite to minimise tension

Stay upwind of your lines to avoid getting any part of your body caught in your lines. When you get to your bar, do not touch your bar, if you hold on to your bar your kite could power up. Do not touch your bar!

- Continue to pull yourself all the way back to your kite
- When you get back to your kite secure it safely with some weight or pack it away immediately.
- While pulling yourself up your safety line back to you kite, stay upwind of the excess lines and avoid getting any part of your body wrapped in the lines.
- Resist the temptation to run back to your kite when it lands. It could blow away at any time. Pull yourself to your kite using your safety line.
- Be prepared to let go of the safety line quickly if your kite does power up for some reason and be prepared to use your final safety release if your kite is pulling you after you have activated your main safety system.

**Practice your self-land on a no wind or light wind day.**

### Self-Landing Made Simple
1. Before you self-land make sure you have two kite line lengths of clear space downwind of you.
2. Move your kite to the edge of the window either at 9 or 3 and activate your safety.
3. Pull yourself back to your kite up the one safety lines using the hand over hand technique, do not touch your bar throughout the whole self-land and continue up the safety line until you have your kite in your hands.

# Trimming your kite

**The main purpose of your kites trim system is to help give you less power.**

You are overpowered if your kite is pulling you when it is in the no power zones at the edges of the wind window at positions 9, 10, 11, 12, 1, 2 or 3. This is when you should pull in your depower trim because doing so will give your kite a little less power.

**Your trim system works by shortening your centre lines so when you pull in your trim system your outside lines become slack. This changes the angle of your kite in the same way as pushing your bar away and**

simply means that your kite does not catch as much wind.

**The downside to pulling in too much trim is that the more you depower your kite, the slacker your steering lines and the less responsive your kite will become.**

Know your trim system as they are all slightly different. Is it a strap? Is it a pulley? Is it spring loaded? Is it a clam cleat? Where is it? Is it above the bar or below the bar? Find out how it works and that it is functioning properly before you fly your kite. Many kites have a colour coding system. Red usually means emergency and should be pulled if you have too much power. Some kites are marked more power and less power.

**As a guide here is how to use your trim system for normal riding**
In strong wind you may want less power so you would pull your depower rope in.
In light wind, if you become underpowered and you could not stand up on the board or stay upwind letting out your depower trim will lengthen your centre lines and tighten your steering lines giving you more power.In extremely light wind to prevent back stalling, pull your depower trim system in all the way towards you for less power. This shortens your centre lines and helps prevent over sheeting which is where the angle of your kite is too aggressive for the strength of the wind resulting in your kite falling from the sky which is called a backstall.

**When trimming your bar, use only small adjustments as maximum depower or maximum power can have a negative effect on your kites performance. Whatever the conditions and as a general rule, most kites work at their best when they have the trim system pulled in a little so your kite has a little depower.**

## Trimming your kite made simple
1. Make sure you understand how your kites depower system works before you fly it.
2. Shorter centre lines mean less power and longer centre lines mean more power.
3. Most kites fly best with a little depower.

# Changing direction while riding

Also known as sliding turns, basic turns, linked turns or most commonly known as transitions. A turn is a controlled stop and then a board start in the opposite direction without sitting down.

As you send your kite through to 12 and are slowing down, push your trailing foot out to slide the back of your board so it is pointing downwind.

As your kite moves through 12 send your kite in the opposite direction and into the power zone, similar to a board start by pulling harder on your opposite hand.

Ride off in the new direction like a normal board start

As you pick up speed, edge harder, lean back and ride upwind.

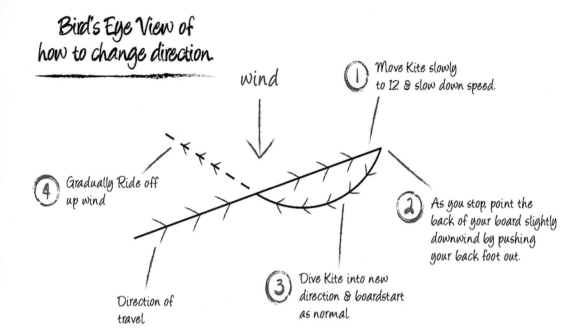

**Bird's Eye View of how to change direction.**

wind

① Move Kite slowly to 12 & slow down speed.

④ Gradually Ride off up wind

② As you stop, point the back of your board slightly downwind by pushing your back foot out.

③ Dive Kite into new direction & boardstart as normal.

Direction of travel.

## Common transition mistakes

- **Mistake** -Trying to go back in exactly the opposite direction.
- **Solution** - Go a little downwind.
- **Mistake** - Sending the kite through the power zone resulting in getting pulled over your front
- **Solution** - Move your kite above your head through 12.
- **Mistake** - Sending the kite too quickly to the other side of the wind window and getting pulled into the air
- **Solution** - Move your kite slowly back to 12 and then into the new direction when you have slowed your riding speed down to almost completely stopping
- **Mistake** - Riding too fast
- **Solution** - Slow down
- **Mistake** - Sinking
- **Solution** - Pull your bar in, dive your kite harder to move it into the power zone.

## Changing direction made simple

1. Practice sliding turns by coming to a controlled stop and then board starting in the opposite direction as soon as you stop.
2. Bring your kite slowly back to 12 and slow right down.
3. Board start in the new direction just before you sink and ride off slightly downwind before leaning back, edging and riding back in the same direction

# Self Rescue

As you are riding further and further away from the safety of the land, if something goes wrong and you cannot relaunch your kite, you must know how to rescue yourself from deep water. A self-rescue is the term used for the technique to safely wind up your lines when in deep water, to get back to your kite and use it as a sailing craft to get back to land.

## When to self-rescue?

- Your kite is down and there is no way to relaunch again because there is no wind.
- Your kite is down because something is broken.
- You are drifting out to sea and there is no way to get back to land by flying your kite.
- You may need to self-rescue at any time and it can happen to can anyone which is why every Kitesurfer needs to know how to self-rescue and be confident to perform it in all conditions.

**There are several different techniques that can be used. The following technique requires the least amount of strength and can be used in all conditions by all riders who have a modern, one line, flag out style safety system. If you have a two line safety system or a**

**five line safety system, check the manufacturer's website for their recommended self-rescue technique.**

- During the self-rescue stay upwind of your lines and make sure that you do not get any part of your body caught in your lines.
- If you have your board, the easiest way to self-rescue with your board is to put your board on your feet.
- In light wind you may have to pull on your safety line to help it pass through your bar to let you kite fully depower.
- When handling any Kitesurfing line, hold the line with your palms facing down using the "hand over hand, thumbs out" technique. This method gives you maximum grip on the line. It also enables you to let go of the line as quickly as possible if your kite powers up and pulls the line from your hands

# Part one – Wrapping your safety line....

- Let go of your bar and activate your safety system.

- Wait until your kite has turned around, your bar has stopped moving up your safety line and there is little or no pull from your kite.

- Pull yourself up your safety line using the palms down, hand over hand, thumbs out technique until you get back to your bar.

- When you get to your bar, you need to stop the kite from powering up while you wind the rest of the lines up. This is a crucial part of the self-rescue and is called locking off.

- As soon as you touch your bar, wrap your safety line around the end of your bar, as quickly and as tightly as possible. The hand action is similar to winding a car window down. This is locking off any unwanted power so you can easily wind the remaining lines on to your bar to get yourself back to your kite.

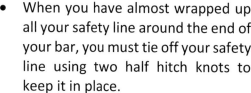
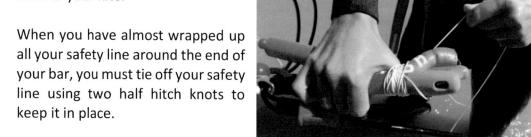

- When you have almost wrapped up all your safety line around the end of your bar, you must tie off your safety line using two half hitch knots to keep it in place.

- To make a half hitch, pinch the line with two fingers and then twist your fingers so the line now makes a loop with the lines crossed over. This is called a half hitch.

- Push the end of your bar through the twisted loop and pull the lines tight. Put in two half hitches twice so there is no chance your safety line can come lose.

- Hold the remaining four lines and wrap them on the bar as tightly as possible the same way as you would pack your lines away normally, end to end, in a figure of eight.

# Self Rescue Part Two – Getting back to your kite

- To make it as easy as possible to wind your lines up and get back to your bar use the fishing pole technique.

- Hold your bar like you would hold a fishing rod with both hands underneath it, one hand in front of the other and with your lines over the end of the bar furthest away from you. Put the end of the bar closest to you on your stomach and pull the bar back like you have caught a big fish. This will create slack in your lines and will make it easier to wind your lines on to your bar.

- Keep wrapping all four lines up as neatly as possible until you are between two to three meters away from your kite. This is an important part of the self-rescue. If you wind all your lines up it will make it very difficult to flip your kite over and turn it into a sail.

**When you are between two and three meters away from your kite you must lock off your lines with two half hitches.**

To make a half hitch hold your hand out with your palm up and grab your lines, pull them towards you to create some slack, turn your palm over to face down and push your bar end through the loop you have just made, then pull your lines tightly and repeat.

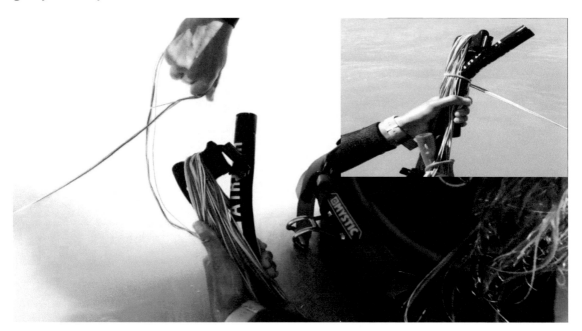

Let go of your bar and pull yourself back to your kite along a centre line using the "hand over hand, thumbs up" technique until you get back to your kite and you can hold on to the main bladder.

# Part Three of self rescue– Turning your kite into a sail boat

- Hold on to your kites main bladder so you are upwind and your kite is down wind of you.

- Move yourself along the main bladder to the wing tip that is nearest the land.

- Face the land and put your shoulder that is closest to your kite, underneath the main bladder.

- Pull the wing tip under the water at the same time as you push with your shoulder and your kite will turn over into the smiley face position.

- With the wind on your back, choose which side of your kite is in the direction of land.

- Move yourself along the main bladder and get hold of the bridle so it makes a handle.

- Keep hold of the bridle and move yourself back to the other end of your kite. This will bend your kite into a C shape that makes a sail pointing toward the land.

- Face the land, hold your bridle with one hand, if you have your board on your feet then now you can take if off and hold it with your other hand as you would if you were body dragging normally with your board.

- Position your legs so they are trailing behind you.

- Be patient as progress can be slow.

# Part four – The full pack down

## When to perform a full pack down

- Only if you are not making any progress back towards the land.
- Only if you have to get through large waves to get back to the land.
- Only if you are 100% sure that you are going to be rescued by a boat.

## How to perform a full deep water pack down

- Before you take out any air from your kite, check that your struts will stay inflated as a kite with no air will sink.
- Most modern kites have valves on the struts that should be clipped shut to prevent the whole kite deflating. Double check that these valves are closed.
- Open your dump valve on your leading edge.
- Keeping your dump valve above water, squeeze as much air out of your main bladder as possible.

- If you can squeeze 90% of the air out of your main bladder your pack down will be much easier.

- Reseal the dump valve to stop any water from getting inside your kite.

- Get your bar and put it inside your kite in line with a strut near the wing tip.

- Roll your kite up as tightly as possible from one wing tip to the other so your kite looks like a sausage.

- Unclip your safety leash on your harness and tie your rolled kite up so it does not unroll.

- You now have an inflatable life raft that you can swim with through waves, back to the land or hand to the kind person in the rescue boat.

If you are rescued at sea by a boat, make sure you thank your rescuers and offer to pay them a small reward for the rescue as according to an ancient international marine law they have salvage rights and can claim your equipment as theirs.

# Practice your self-rescue and pack down on a no wind day in safe, shallow water or on the land. You will not regret it and it could save your life one day.

### Self-Rescue & deep water pack down made simple

- Avoid a self-rescue by conducting and effective wind and site assessment every time you go Kitesurfing. Avoid marginal conditions, If in doubt, dont go out.
- Release your safety, wind your safety line around the end of your bar, lock off your safety line, wind yourself back to your kite, turn your kite over, hold a bridle, bend your kite over into a C shape position and face the land.
- Only perform a full pack down if you have no other way of getting back to the land

*"Practice your self-rescue and emergency pack down! You probably learnt it on day one of your lessons but that can feel like a distant memory so it is well worth going through it on your own on a light wind day. As a beginner you should stick to beaches where you can put your feet down but you never know when you might need to use your self-rescue skills. As you progress and Kitesurf at different locations with waves and deeper water you still may never need to use it but if you have to, the confidence you'll have from knowing you've practiced it will make the difference between a potential "kitemare" and a casual sail to the beach! Apart from that smile, enjoy and welcome to the family!"* **Matt Bellamy BIG Kite Rider UK**

# Light Wind Riding

Knowing how to set up and fly your kite in light wind can mean the difference between having the best session of your life or having a total "kitemare". In light winds there is a much smaller room for error so your technique has to be spot on.

## "Golden" light wind trick and tips

- Modern, top quality kites have much better relaunching capabilities which is one of the many reasons why they are more expensive.
- Line extensions extend the wind range of your kite helping your kite to fly and have more power in light wind.
- Pump your kite up as hard as you dare in light wind so it is as rigid as possible.
- Only go out as far as you are prepared to swim.
- Light wind requires much more movement of your kite from more aggressive movement of your bar.
- If the wind starts to drop or the wind changes in anyway and your kite becomes difficult to control, get back to the safety of the land immediately.
- If the wind stops suddenly move your kite around as fast as you can as it will create its own wind which will help it to stay in the sky.
- In light wind, the wind window is smaller. To help keep your kite in the sky keep your kite high between 11 and 1. Any lower towards the edges of the wind window and your kite may fall out of the sky.
- Focus on keeping your kite up as relaunching in very light wind can be difficult or even impossible.
- Learn how to down loop your kite to keep it in the air. This is where you dive your kite towards the sea so it picks up speed and can be used if the wind drops suddenly or if

you move your kite too far to the edge of the window and you lose control. Study the down looping section in this book to learn how to downloop safely.

- If you cannot stay upwind, stop and walk back. Don't risk one more ride out to try and find wind. It's better to be on the land wishing you were on the water than on the water wishing you were on the land.
- Always try to relaunch your kite towards the land if possible so you are not pulled further out to sea while you are launching.

# Light wind setup

The best advice you will ever hear for riding in light wind is to set your kite up for Low power!

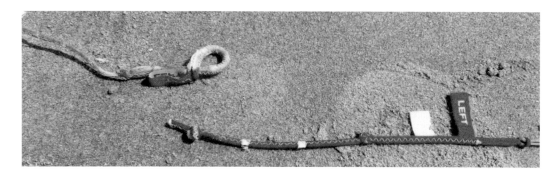

**Yes, low power. The opposite of what most people think. This is to help prevent back stalling which can happen to all kites in light wind. *Back stalling is when the angle of your kite is too great for the wind to support it. It is caused by the kite being trimmed for maximum power and then when you pull your bar in your kite simply falls backwards.***

## To minimise this happening

- Connect your steering lines to the knot that is furthest away from your kite. Sometimes this is marked low power.
- Pull in your kite trim system to shorten your centre lines enough so when you pull your bar in your kite is not fully powered or over sheeting. An over sheeted kite is when the angle is too great so the shape becomes inefficient; to spot this when you pull your bar in fully usually the ends of the kite will flare out slightly.
- These settings also work extremely well for all other wind speeds and most experienced riders have their steering lines connected to the knots that are furthest away from the kite all the time.

### Light wind riding made simple

1. Know that in light wind your kite should be setup for low power and be depowered, yes less power in light wind.
2. Know that the wind window is smaller in light winds and your kite can drop out of the sky from any lower than 11 or 1.
3. Focus on keeping your kite in the air as relaunching in light wind can be impossible, remember that your kite is the most important component of Kitesurfing, keep it moving or down loop it if is falling out of the sky.

# Understanding Back stalling

If your kite falls backwards toward the ground in the opposite direction of how it is usually fly's then this is called a back stall. It's the same principle as an aircraft stall. It is very common in light wind and with poorly set up kites. You can minimise it happening by setting your kite up for low power but it can still happen so what do you do if it does happen? As soon as your kite starts to fall backwards towards the water you must

immediately.......... **PUSH YOUR BAR OUT**

This is the opposite of what most people expect and the opposite of what your instructor has been telling you throughout your lessons so it's a lot to understand.

Pushing your bar away as soon as a back stall happens will help your kite to catch the wind and fly properly again. You must keep your bar pushed away until your kite rises back up to the no power zone. You may have to push your bar all the way out and as your kite begins to fly again you may get pulled as it will be in the power zone.

As soon as your kite begins to lift back up you then must get back in control, pull your bar back in and and fly your kite as normal.

**Back stalling made simple**
1. Remember to set your kite and trim system up for less power to prevent back stalling in light wind.
2. As soon as your kite falls backwards push your bar away.
3. Fly your kite back up to 12 as soon as possible

# Light wind relaunching

Relaunching your kite from the water in light wind is much more technical and challenging especially when you have less experience. It is extremely important to know how to relaunch your kite in light wind if you are in deep water otherwise you will be performing a lot of unnecessary self-rescues. Your top tips are.....

- Be patient.
- Use a steering line, not your bar. This will help you to avoid back stalling your kite.
- Be gentle. Extremely gentle. Release the tension immediately as your kite launches from the water.
- Launch your kite more in front of you, in the middle of the power zone. This will help you to get your kite up into the C shape position because your kite is catching more wind in the power zone. Remember, this only applies in light wind when you are in the water.

If you have no success and your kite is still in the water, try something different such as letting go of your bar, pulling on another line, swimming backwards, pulling even more gently or pulling on the centre lines to help it flip over.

**Remember the famous Einstein quote "Insanity is doing the same thing over and over again and expecting a different result".**

# Hot launching

A hot launch is where you launch your kite in the middle of the power zone when your kite has its leading edge facing towards the sky. It's called a hot launch because when it launches it is in the middle of the power zone and you will be pulled forwards potentially with great force.

**Only hot launch in light winds when you are in water, never attempt a hot launch while you are in shallow water below the knee or on the land. You can only hot launch when your kite is directly downwind of you, has its leading edge out of the water and the struts are pointing to 12.**

**Only when your kite is in this position can you do the following, in sequence….**

- Let go of your bar or push it out as far as possible.
- Pull hard on the centre lines.
- Swim backwards and pull hard on your centre lines if necessary.
- Wait until your kite rises clear from the water and do not touch your bar until it does.
- Prepare for some power and to be pulled though the water.
- Get hold of your bar and move your kite to 12 as soon as possible.

# Down looping your kite

Why downloop? In extreme light wind, if you have moved your kite too far past 11 or 1 there is a good chance that there will not be enough wind to hold your kite in the air and it will fall out of the sky. If your kite becomes totally unresponsive in the sky, you can force a down loop to keep your kite in the sky and to move it back into the power.

Down looping drives your kite down so it picks up speed, creates its own wind and becomes more responsive. It's the same principle as an aeroplane that is stalling and needs to be sent into a dive for the pilot to regain control. Down loops should only be practiced in super light wind.

## How to down loop?

**Important! Practice only in very light wind in shallow water above your knee and with several hundred meters of space downwind of you.**

Take your kite to 11 or 1 at the edge of the wind window before you down loop. Don't down loop in the middle of the power zone.

Pull your bar in all the way to the stopper so you have full power and maximum responsiveness. If your kite is on your left, pull as hard as you can on the left side of your bar. **Keep pulling on the one side of your bar, hard. Keep pulling until your kite turns all the way around and starts to climb back up to 12.**

- If your kite is not turning fast enough with your bar pulled in all the way, you can pull the steering line to help it to turn more quickly.
- Prepare for some power.
- Push your bar away if you feel a surge of power as it travels back up through the middle of the power zone or hold on and get body dragged but keep flying your kite.
- Only let go of your bar if you are in danger.
- **Bring your kite to 12.**
- Your lines will be twisted. Do not panic. Fly your kite as normal.
- You can fly your kite with twisted lines as long as you keep the red or the left side of your bar on your left.
- When your kite has settled and is at 12 then you can unspin your bar calmly.

If you attempt a down loop and your kite is too low in the window such as at 10 or 2, you could be too late and no matter how hard you pull your bar end or even your line, your kite may not have enough room to turn fully and climb back up before hitting the water.

# The Downloop

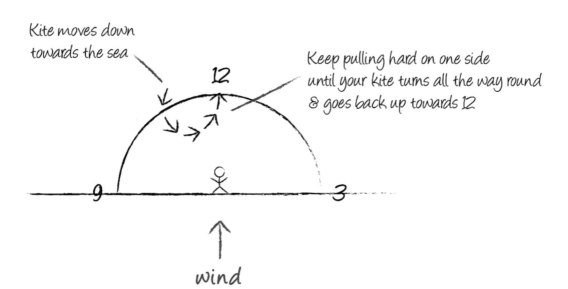

Kite moves down towards the sea

12

Keep pulling hard on one side until your kite turns all the way round & goes back up towards 12

9

3

wind

**Know that the harder you pull your bar, the quicker your kite will turn through the down loop and the less that you will get pulled.**

**Downlooping your kite made simple**
1. Only down loop your kite as a last resort and when it is at the edge of the wind window where there is less power
2. If your kite is on your right pull hard on the right side of your bar, if your kite is on your left, pull hard on the left side of your bar.
3. Do not twist your bar, keep it level and keep pulling hard until your kite turns all the way around

# Twisted lines, inverted kites and putting your safety back together under tension.

While in the learning stages of Kitesurfing you will inevitably be crashing your kite more often. The more you crash your kite, the greater the chance that you will twist your lines or that your kite will invert. There is also a chance that you could accidently activate your main safety and if any of this happens while you are in deep water, you need to know how to fix it and get back to the safety of the land.

### Putting your safety back together under tension in the water
Firstly make sure that you have a modern, one line safety system, so when your main safety system has been activated, you have as little power as possible.
Secondly it is crucial that you know how your safety system works before you go out. Practice putting your safety system back together on the land when it is not attached to your kite so you are confident enough to be able to put it back together in the water.

### To put your safety back together so you can fly your kite again, follow these steps

When your safety has been released you will be attached to your kite by your safety line.

- Pull yourself up your safety line using the palms down, hand over hand, thumbs up technique. This is the same technique to handle your lines as the self-rescue and the self land.

- Pull yourself all the way back to your bar

**Make sure you stay upwind of the excess line so you do not get tangled.**

When you get back to your bar, avoid holding your bar and letting go of your safety line. When you hold on to your bar, your kite will start to catch the wind and pull your safety line back through your bar.

This means that your kite could power up aggressively, very quickly. This would be dangerous because the excess line could get caught around a part of your body or another piece of your equipment. You would also be fully powered while be holding your bar without being connected to your harness.

**When you put your safety system back together you will need to continue holding on to your safety line.**

If you cannot put your safety system back together with one hand while you are holding on to your safety line, you can secure your safety line by wrapping it around your spreader bar on your harness two or three times.

This will prevent your safety line from being pulled back though your bar while you reload your safety and will free up both hands to put your safety back together. Be cautious when unwrapping the line from your hook.

- When your safety system is back together, hook your chicken loop into your spreader bar and put your chick stick through the bottom of your spreader bar to secure it in place as normal.

- When your safety is properly put back together and you are hooked back in, let the excess safety line back through your bar as slowly as possible.

- Be prepared to let go of your safety line at any moment if your kite powers up and the safety line starts being pulled through your hands
- Relaunch your kite as normal.

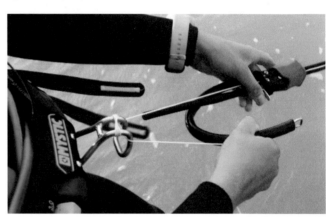

If there is a large amount of tension and you struggle to hold on to your safety line, bar or

chicken loop at any time you must remember to simply...... **let go!**

Remember that you have the option of performing a self-rescue if you can not put your safety back together. As a further option, if you are not far from the land and your kite is at the edge of the wind window towards the land, you can swim back if you swim upwind from your lines.

 *"Be aware of your surroundings; with all the fun you are having while riding on the board, body dragging or even just drifting in the water, it is very easy to lose track of where you are as you will cover a lot of ground very quickly. It is important to keep your distance from other Kitesurfers and beach goers but also try to make sure you do not ride off to far, stay close enough to everyone else in case you need help or someone to land your kite."* **Thomas Cawte – Owner, Senior Instructor thekitesurfcentre.co.uk**

### Putting your safety back together made simple

1.  Use the palms down, thumbs out, hand over hand method to get back to your safety system making sure you stay upwind of your lines so you do not get any body parts tangled in your safety line.
2.  Do not let go of your safety line when putting your safety back together or hold on to your bar or chicken loop as your safety line could move through your safety system with great speed and power up your kite. Consider wrapping your safety line around your spreader bar hook to take the tension off while you reload your safety system.
3.  When your safety is back together feed the safety line back through as slowly as possible.

# Twisted lines

**If your kite lines have become twisted then do not panic**! You can fly your kite as normal with twisted lines **as long as your bar is the right way round with the red side on your left.**
If you have down looped your kite or accidently spun around when you crashed then you can simply unspin your bar and your lines will be untwisted.
If your kite crashed, it may have twisted itself through your lines and even when you unspin your bar your lines may still be twisted, again don't panic.
Keep your bar the right way round and fly your kite as normal. You can ride or body drag as normal back to the land to fix them.

**It is highly recommended that you only fly your kite with twisted lines for as long as it takes to get back to the land where you can land or self-land to untwist your lines, relaunch and then go back out.**

The safest and most often the quickest way to untangle your lines is to land and secure your kite, untie your lines, lay them out downwind behind your kite and untwist them in the same way as if you were setting up your kite at the beginning.
If your lines have twisted around your kite, then your kite could get damaged or become dangerous if relaunched and you must activate your main safety before you attempt to relaunch your kite.

**After riding for some time your centre lines can become twisted. For most systems this is not a problem but some systems, when the centre lines are twisted multiple times, the effectiveness when activating the main safety system can be severely compromised or even fail to release. When you setup your kite always untwist your centre lines before you launch and it is wise to keep your centre lines untwisted all the time you are flying your kite. Know your centre line system and know how to untwist it while your kite is in the sky. This could actually save your life if you had to use your safety in a real emergency.**

Every kite brand is different but most kites have some sort of spinning centre line system to help prevent your centre lines from twisting. Most modern systems can be untwisted by twisting the lines above the chicken loop the opposite way, using one hand while your kite is at 12.

# Twisted lines made simple

1. You can fly your kite with twisted lines as long as your bar is the right way round.
2. Get back to the land as soon as you can and untwist your lines.
3. Activate your main safety and self-rescue if your lines become tangled and your kite is not flying properly.

# Dealing with an Inverted Kite

An inverted kite is where your kite turns inside out. It will look strange and it is easy to tell that something is wrong because its shape will change.

The kite at the top is inverted and the to the left is normal

To minimise the chances of your kite inverting, make sure you pump your kite up so it is hard. A softer kite will invert more easily. A harder kite has more chance of retaining its shape. If your kite does invert while you are in deep water, you have several options.

## Firstly know that you can still fly your kite if it inverts.

It won't perform as normal but if you are able to relaunch it, you can body drag with your board back to the beach where you can land or self-land to fix it. Do not attempt to ride with an inverted kite as this could cause damage, especially in strong wind. When body dragging, keep your kite at the edge of the wind window, in the no power zone.

If you cant fly your inverted kite, it is possible to fix it without body dragging back to land by gently crashing it into the water. This is risky because you could damage your kite and is not guaranteed to work.

If you cannot launch your kite, pull on the line that will move your kite towards the land so you are pulled back slowly towards the land.

If your kite will not relaunch and you are not getting back to land then you will have to activate your safety system. This will mean that your kite will lose tension, spin around and regain its proper shape but you will then have to put your safety back together while you are in the water so make sure you are confident to put your safety back together in strong wind and in deep water.

**If you cannot launch your kite or fix the invert and you have tried everything, if you are not drifting back to the land then it time to activate your main safety system and perform a self-rescue.**

If you can successfully fix your inverted kite then it is highly likely that your lines will be crossed over and twisted. Remember that as long as you have your bar the correct way around usually with the red side on your left, you will be able to fly your kite as normal even though your lines may look strange to get back to the beach where you can land your kite and untwist your lines.

## Dealing with an inverted kite made simple
1. Pump your kite up extremely hard to help prevent an invert.
2. If you are in deep water, know that you can fly your kite inverted and body drag with your board back to shallow water or to the land to fix it.
3. Activating your main safety and then reloading it usually fives the invert but be prepared to self land or self rescue if this doesn't work.

# Self-launching

Self-launching is when you launch your kite on your own, without an assistant and on the land. It is a simple procedure if performed properly in a safe environment, with modern equipment and with a little practice but it is not advised unless you are extremely confident with your water relaunching and general kite flying skills.

**The following technique is for a modern kite with high depower and is not to be used with old kites that have little depower or C shaped kites.**

If there were only one important point to remember about the self-launch it would be this.......

**DO NOT TOUCH YOUR BAR**

- If you do not touch your bar throughout the self-launch then there is almost no possibility that your kite could power up and pull you over.
- However, If you are pulled and you are not touching your bar then simply activate your safety system.

## When should you self-launch?

When there is no one around you that can assist you to launch. Remember Kitesurfing on your own can be dangerous. If there is no one else Kitesurfing, ask yourself some basic questions like why is there no one Kitesurfing here? Is it safe to Kitesurf at this location? Is the wind good enough? Are my skills good enough for the wind and the location?

## Do not self-launch if

- You do not have at least two kite line lengths or 50 meters of space between you and any dangerous obstacles such as rocks, walls, people, boats, roads or anything else that could injure you or your kite if you hit them.
- The surface that you will be standing and launching on has sharp stones or rocks that can damage you or your kite.
- You are not 100% confident in your kite flying skills.

## Self-launching preparations

- Carry out a wind and site assessment as normal to be absolutely sure of your safety.
- The best surface for a self-launch is sand but a pebble beach is sufficient if the stones are round and not sharp although it is not ideal, it is possible to self-launch on stones.
- Be sure that you choose the right size kite.
- Set your kite up as normal with your lines running downwind from your kite.
- Double check your entire setup.
- Double check that all your lines and bridles are untwisted.
- Double check that you have connected your lines to your kite correctly and to the correct knots.
- Double check that your main and final safety release are all working by activating them and putting them back together before you launch.
- Visualise your launch as normal. You will be launching your kite as normal at the edge of the wind window at a right angle to the wind direction. To be sure, stand with your back to the wind and put your arms out to your side. Whichever hand is pointing towards the water is the direction and the angle that you will be launching from.
- Plan to launch your kite as close to the water as possible.
- Plan to launch so your kite is facing the water so if you have too much power you are pulled towards the water and not towards the land.
- Put your board upwind of you and near the water so it does not get in the way and is easy to pick up when you have launched.

# How to Self-launch

When you have completed all your preparations and are 100% confident that you have at least fifty meters of space downwind of you and you have double checked your setup:

- Secure your kite with just enough weight to hold it on the ground so that it does not move while you walk back to your bar. If you put too much weight on your kite, the self-launch will be difficult and could even be dangerous. A weighted bag is ideal but loose sand will do. In strong wind, loose sand can be blown from your kite and your kite could be blown away. To minimise this happening put a little extra sand on your kite in strong wind and walk quickly back to your bar.

- When you get back to your bar, hook your safety leash in first.
- Hook your chicken loop in to your spreader bar and secure it in place with your chick stick as normal.
- Remember not to touch your bar during any part of the self-launch.

- Walk backwards until your lines have a little tension.

- You can put a hand near your safety system so you can activate it quickly if something goes wrong or you feel nervous.

- Start walking slowly into the wind while keeping a little tension in your lines

- As you walk further into the wind, your kite will start to turn around. As it turns, slow your walking pace down and just take one step at a time and continue to resist the urge to touch your bar.

- Each step you take your kite will turn more and more into the wind and fill with air until the weight that you put on starts to slide off.

- Untwist your lines if they are twisted by spinning your bar but don't hold your bar.
- Your kite will pivot on its wing tip and start to turn on its side, into the C shape position just as it would when you are relaunching on the water.
- Pull gently on the steering line until your kite slowly leaves the ground and stays at the edge of the wind window in the no power zone.

- Keep pulling very gently on your steering line until your kite is near 12.
- Get hold of your bar and fly your kite as normal. Note: it is wise to fly your kite with one hand and keep your kite below 11 or 1 while you are on the land.
- Pick up your board and get into the water as soon as possible.

**What to do if anything goes wrong during a self-launch.**

- If you have accidently pulled your bar, let go of it immediately.
- Activate your main safety system.
- Sit down on the ground if you are being pulled so are not pulled over
- Activate your final safety if your kite is still pulling you.

# Self-launching Made Simple

1. Make sure you have fifty meters of clear space on a soft surface, double check your setup, launch towards the sea at a right angle to the wind in the no power zone either at 9 or 3.
2. Put on just enough weight to secure your kite, walk back to your bar, connect safety systems, do not touch your bar throughout the whole self-launch until your kite is safely in the sky.
3. Walk backwards to keep tension in your lines then walk into the wind until your kite catches the wind and turns in to the C shape, pull gently on the steering line attached to the wing tip in the air until your kite is off the ground in the same way you would launch your kite in the water.

# The Death loop

A death loop is an extremely rare event in Kitesurfing and the chances are it will never happen to you. However, it can happen and there is a good reason why it's called the death loop so you need to know what to do if it does happens to you.

**What is it exactly?** A death loop is where your kite keeps looping and spinning around, out of control in the power zone. The result is that you can get pulled through the water or on the land with great force.

## How could it happen?
- A kite line or bridle gets twisted around the wing tip of the kite.
- The lines get twisted around the bar.
- The lines become twisted or tangled in a certain way.
- One or more of the lines has snapped or there is some other type of equipment failure.
- The bar gets caught on the spreader bar hook.
- Something gets wrapped in the lines.

## How to minimise it happening
- Avoid riding with old lines or kites.
- Know how to activate your main safety and your final safety with your eyes closed.
- Always carry a line cutter.
- Attach your final safety quick release to your predominant side or to the front of your harness so it is quick and easy to activate, for example, if you are right handed, attach your leash to the right hand side of your harness. Never ride with your safety leash attached behind you on your harness handle.
- Avoid Kitesurfing in strong winds.
- Check your gear for any signs of wear every time you set up. Never ride with worn or damaged equipment, if in doubt don't go out.
- Do not ride if you find a knot in any of your lines and if you can untie the knot be careful not to damage your line.
- Always perform a pre-flight check before you launch your kite to make sure that you have connected your lines to the right parts of your kite and activate both your main and final safety systems to be 100% sure that they work.
- Check that your bridles are not twisted over a wingtip before you give the thumbs up to launch your kite.
- Let go of your bar every time you crash your kite.
- Avoid getting anything caught in your lines.
- If you crash your kite while riding, don't ride over your lines, turn away from your kite.

## What can you do if it happens?

- First of all let go and activate your main safety.
- If you are still being pulled release your final safety immediately.
- What if I can't activate my safety?
- You can force your kite to back stall and stop looping by pulling one of your steering lines as hard as you can until your kite stops moving. Any steering line will do but the one closest to the kite will stop your kite the quickest. This technique is only recommended if you cannot activate your main safety.
- Use your line cutter as a last resort to cut your lines.

## The Death Loop Made Simple

1. Check that your bridles are not twisted around your wing tips when launching.
2. Know that activating your main safety is the first thing to do, know how to activate your safety system and how to get to your line cutter with your eyes closed.
3. If your main safety will not open you can force a back stall and stop the death loop by pulling hard on a steering line, preferably the one furthest away from you.

# Buying Equipment

When the wind is constant, the sun is shining and you have perfect flat water or the perfect waves, you do not want to miss a session because your equipment has let you down. If your Kitesurfing equipment is top quality, well looked after and up to date, you will progress faster, with greater ease, more safely ultimately making your whole experience much more enjoyable. The better your gear, the less chance that it could let you down. In short in you buy the right equipment and look after it.

## The most important part of your equipment is your kite.

- Go for Delta, hybrid, bow or bridled open C shaped kites. Most new kites on the market fall into these categories.
- Avoid C shaped or high aspect kites, also avoid five line kites or bars if you are relatively new to Kitesurfing, leave them to experienced riders who want to perform specific things.
- Go for the largest and most established brands, they have the most experience in the production of Kitesurfing kites. They know what kite designs perform the best and how to make their kites durable. Spare parts will be more widely available which is especially useful if you are on holiday.

- The bestselling kites are all very similar and offer the ability to do almost everything. Popular kites and brands are popular because they work well and are reliable.
- Don't believe everything that you read on forums. If you want individual advice, speak to your instructor or an experienced Kitesurfer.
- Avoid any kite that is aimed at learners and schools as you will outgrow it too quickly.
- An all-round kite is a very sensible option.
- Brand new kites are said to have magical powers.
- Beware of new kites that are much cheaper than all the other kites. You get what you pay for. Cheap Kitesurfing gear is cheap for a reason.

## Buying a second hand kite

- Go for as new as possible. The latest gear has the latest safety systems and the latest designs that will make it easier for you to fly and to relaunch.
- Do not buy any kite that is old. Kites before 2007 were terrible in comparison to today's kites as well having dangerous safety systems such as wrist leashes. Don't be tempted even if it's cheap or in as new condition.
- Old kites can be like old cars and have lots of problems such as slow leaks or and be more prone to ripping if crashed on the water. Old lines are more likely to snap.
- Make sure your kite has a one line safety system. Avoid kites or bars with two line safety systems as they are not safe to self-rescue in strong winds because they still have some power when you release your main safety.
- If you do decide buy second hand, a sensible option is to buy from a reputable shop who have checked the equipment over.
- Beware of buying ex school kites unless they are extremely new and from a reputable school with a clear system to look after their kites.

## What to check for and how to know it's time to change your equipment.
**Some common signs that a kite has been well used and needs replacing.**
- The kite has faded colours.
- The canopy is soft, is not shiny and does not make a loud rustling or crispy noise when you take it out of the bag.
- There are fold marks on the trailing edge.
- The kite loses air.
- There is lose, frayed stitching in any area of the kite.
- There are poor repairs where material overlaps or the stitching is not neat and tidy like the factory stitching.
- Don't be put off by kites that have been repaired professionally. A repaired kite should be slightly cheaper but if the repair has been done professionally then it will make no noticeable difference when flying the kite and can actually make the kite stronger.

# Buying a Wetsuit

- Warmth and flexibility are key. Kitesurfing when you are cold is not fun and it can be dangerous. Many riders wear a 4/5mm wetsuit in most cool water locations or a thin shorty suit even in the warmest waters. Generally, the more expensive the suit the more flexible it is.
- For extra warmth, semi dry suits have a soft, furry inside which provide exceptional comfort and warmth. You may feel a little warm on the beach or when you are riding but how warm will you be if you have to perform a self-rescue and are in the water for hour at the end of your session when you are tired?
- Spend as much as you can on your wetsuit, it will be great investment. Pay double the price and buy half as many. More expensive wetsuits keep you warmer, are more flexible, last longer and are more comfortable. Some even come with a lifetime guarantee.
- Established brands generally make the best wetsuits.
- If you can, try before you buy. Your suit should have a snug fit and be comfortable. Over time and when in the water your suit will stretch. Check that you are happy getting in to your suit on your own, front zips can be difficult to get in and out of on your own but offer the most warmth and comfort and you will get used to putting it on over a little time. Wetsuits with rear zips are the easiest and quickest to get into but cold water can trickle down the back if your suit does not fit properly.

# Buying a Harness

- A waist harness is the most popular harness style used. Seat harnesses only tend to be used by beginners on their first few lessons and by people with different body shapes.
- If you can, try before you buy. Comfort and fitting is the priority. Different brands have different shapes and sizes, try as many as you can.
- Long established brands are usually the most durable and will last the longest.
- Simple systems are the strongest and the most reliable.
- Your harness should fit you without having to be extremely tight.

# Buying Safety equipment

- Wearing a helmet is extremely sensible. At a busy location someone could crash into you without you seeing them. A helmet can save your life by preventing head injuries and the worst case scenario, becoming unconscious in the water.
- Impact vests are a worthwhile investment giving some protection from hitting the water, they also help keep you warm and offer a little extra buoyancy.

- Boots, gloves and a neoprene hat will keep you warm in extreme cold. They will also offer extra protection. Research shows that you can trick your body into feeling warm by keeping your hands and feet warm.
- For extreme cold wear a windproof, water jacket, they are an amazing solution for keeping warm in extreme cold.

# Buying a Board

- Only buy and use a board that is designed for Kitesurfing.
- The size of your board depends on your size or weight.
- Larger boards help you ride upwind more easily and perform better in lighter winds.
- A good size board for most riders is around 140cm x 40cm.
- A lighter board doesn't necessarily mean a better board.
- Foot straps and pads that fit and are comfortable are as important as the board itself.
- If possible, try before you buy, if you cannot ride in the water at least check that the foot straps are comfortable, fit properly and do not rub.
- It is better to buy a top of the range second hand board than a budget new board.
- Avoid fixed wake style boots when you are learning or are new to Kitesurfing.
- New pads and foot straps can dramatically change how a board feels.

### Buying equipment made simple

1. Invest as much as you can in your equipment but know that you can get quality second hand equipment from a reputable shop.
2. The quality of your equipment has a direct impact on the quality of your Kitesurfing experience as well as the speed of your progression.
3. Your Kite is the most important piece of equipment followed by your personal protective gear and lastly your board. Make your purchase decisions based on where you will Kitesurf the most.

# Equipment Maintenance

If you look after your equipment properly, it will last many years.

## How to look after your kite

- Don't leave it on the beach in the sunshine longer than fifteen minutes – Sun damage makes kites lose their protective shiny coat which weakens the material and absorbs water making your kite more likely to rip and be heavier to fly.
- Secure your kite with sand or even better weighted bags – Do not weigh your kite down with stones or rocks as they will tear your canopy.
- Put your board on your kite with the fins up – Fins will slice through your kite and so will the sharp edges of your board if your kite is flapping. Only put your board on your kite with the foot straps touching the material and your fins in the air.
- Don't leave your kite flapping on the beach – A flappy Kite is truly an unhappy kite. Similar to a flag ripping in strong winds your kite will do the same if left flapping.
- Dry your kite off before putting it away – Fresh water can go mouldy and weaken stitching. Kites are designed for use in salt water and do not need washing with fresh water although it won't hurt it from time to time.
- Brush off all sand before putting it away – Dry sand in your kite bag is like sand paper and will weaken your kites protective coating as well as the material.

## How to look after all your other Kitesurfing equipment

- Rinse all your gear other than your kite in fresh water after every session.
- Avoid using detergent. If you must use a detergent, use a weak solution.
- Dry your equipment out of the sun.
- Hang your wetsuit by folding it in half and laying it over a line. If you have to use a hanger, use a fat hanger. Thin hangers stretch wetsuits.
- General Kitesurfing equipment maintenance
- Keep your pump as clean and as free from sand as possible by keeping it in a bag.
- Lubricate the shaft of your pump and the rubber insides with margarine as it does not wear the rubber out or attract so much dirt and sand.
- If you have a depower rope that is not covered by rubber or plastic you can prolong its life by rubbing candle wax on it. The waxed rope will help your bar to move more smoothly up and down creating less friction and less wear. If your depower rope is fraying, do not risk flying your kite, replace it immediately.

- Board screws come loose over time. If your pads, straps or fins become loose and break free you could injure yourself. Tighten all screws on your board every other session to be sure but be careful not to overtighten or cross thread any screws as doing so could ruin your board.

**It is incredibly useful to always carry a simple tool kit in one of your kite bags with the following equipment**

- A flat head and a cross head screwdriver
- Kite patches for repairing small tears
- A knife
- Multipurpose glue
- Gaffer tape
- Spare fins and spare screws
- A basic first aid kit and some emergency water
- When traveling, take replacement bladders, lines and a spare bar if possible.

## Equipment maintenance made simple

- Check all your equipment before every session as you set up for any signs of wear such as knots in the lines, tears in your kite or fraying lines, ropes or pigtails. Repair or replace immediately. Tighten up your board screws every week.
- Don't pack your kite away if it is wet or has any sand on it and never leave your kite in the sun for more than 15 minutes or flapping in the wind longer than absolutely necessary.
- Rinse and dip if possible, all other equipment with fresh water after each session making sure all sand has been removed.

# Rider Advice Part 2

What one piece of advice would you give to a new Kitesurfer who has just finished their lessons………

*"Make the effort to get out on the water as much as possible, keep all the information fresh and give continuity to the learning process. In the early stages of learning, if there's a big gap in your practice, some things are lost and with that you may not feel as comfortable to go kiting on your own. So no matter how cold it is outside, or if the wind is too light, whatever the reason that might be stopping you from going out, overcome it!" **Bruna Kajiya – Professional Kitesurfer World Freestyle Champion brunakajiya.com.br***

"Welcome to the greatest of sports! Don't forget it can be a dangerous sport, particularly at the beginning. Situations that are dangerous can occur anytime but be particularly careful in your first 30 or so water days. This is when you're trying new stuff all the time and you're not quite aware of your skills and limitations. Make sure you go out with other experienced Kitesurfers and don't be scared to ask for advice. After having practiced self-rescue and self-landed a few times you'll be much safer, feel safer and have much more confidence. Lastly don't drop your kite in the waves. Just don't do it. Now go and enjoy the steep learning curve ahead of you, you are going to have so much fun!!!" **Patrick Stein-Kaempfe Kitesurfing Financial advisor Cape Town**

"Your lessons are your first steps of your Kitesurfing adventure but you still have many, many more adventures to come so find a safe Kitesurfing spot close to your home or move closer to one. Next get some quality equipment. Keep in touch with your instructor, practice, practice, practice and last of all, keep calm and carry on Kitesurfing ;)" **Adham Ahmer International Kitesurfing Instructor Somer bay, Egypt and thekitesurfcentre.com UK**

"Safety has to come first. Accidents in Kitesurfing can and do happen, so get lots of classes before you go out on your own and make sure you know how to kite safely" **Matteo Lombardi - International Kitesurfing Entrepreneur**

"Kitesurfing is enormously fun, addictive and a relatively safe sport nowadays, but there is still one part which causes 90% of all accidents and injuries - the launch. However, with the correct training and pre-flight checks these can all be avoided. So, here are 6 key steps which should be followed every time you go out, and will make your entry into the Kitesurfing world a whole lot safer. It's really important to make sure  the launch area is big enough and clear of dangerous obstructions. You need to be prepared for the worst case scenario, which would be getting dragged downwind into something hard, so you should leave as much space possible in front of you, ideally a minimum of two line lengths. This is also for the protection of your kite should it crash down into something or somebody. Double check that your kite is rigged correctly before asking someone for a launch. It's very easy to have a bridle tangled through itself or a line attached to the wrong place. This has caused fatal accidents in the past and takes just 2 minutes to be sure, even if it means you're the last one on the water. Activate your chicken loop safety release before hooking into your harness. If you have to use it, you need to be sure that it will go off properly when required. Once in the launch position and ready for flight, check your lines are all the same tension and aren't caught around a wingtip, strut end or the bar before it is released. It's easy for this to happen as the kite is turned over to be launched. If something isn't correct it will feel strange on the bar and the kite will probably be trying to pull to the left or right. Launching the kite shouldn't be a fight with the bar, just gentle control and steering, if it isn't then something isn't right. Depower the kite if you feel it's necessary with the adjustment at the bar, as you want the kite launching with as little power and most control possible.

*Finally, as your launching assistant releases the kite, steer it up very slowly rather than swinging it wildly. If there is a problem which has gone unnoticed you can bring it straight back down again without losing control, but hopefully all is well and you can proceed to the water and enjoy the session"* **Tristan Cawte – Owner, Senior Instructor, TheKitesurfCentre Camber Sands UK Thekitesurfcentre.co.uk**

*"Be Patient. Practice Makes Perfect! In the beginning you may feel overwhelmed and keep failing a lot, most new things that you try in Kitesurfing are only a matter of kite control, timing and body position which you can nail by practicing over and over again, don't despair, it eventually all works out and is very much worth all the work."*

**Selin Sohtorik - Kitesurfing Interior Designer Turkey**

*"Kiting will change your life, just be patient when you are in the learning process as like anything new it's all about practice, practice and practice. Always remember the danger of launching a kite in a new spot, with a new wind direction or with different wind strengths. Always be 100% focused from the moment you pump up your kite, connect your lines and give the ok for launching. You always need to be aware that things could go wrong and you ALWAYS need to be*

*ready to use your quick release for avoiding major problems"* **Adrian Fefer - International Kitesurfing Instructor**

*"Make sure you can always swim back, don't go out further than you are prepared to swim. Do a first aid course too as one day you might get in a situation where your help could save someone's life"* **Astrid Jansen – Wave Kitesurfing Legend, Cologne Germany**

*"Get yourself paired up with a great 'KB' (kite buddy)! - You may not realise it initially but finding a new kite buddy to share your beginner experiences and encourage you (not to mention to kite with) is the first step to joining a great community of kiters. It might be a good idea to set the kite up together, take turns with the kite while your buddy launches and lands you, hands you the board, and is generally there for you while you are still unsure of yourself. Then of course you can do the same for them and you'll have someone to drink beers with and talk about Kitesurfing for hours after! ;)"* **Caroline Morris - Progression Sports Kitesurfing training videos Progressionsports.me**

*"When you finish your lessons it's not about being able to Kitesurf well It's about being able to look after yourself well... the rest will follow!"* **David Furney - International Kitesurfing and Sailing Instructor**

*"Be friendly and make some Kitesurfing friends. Hook up with a group of local Kitesurfing buddies for safety, logistics, learning progression and most*  *importantly it's because it's FUN to Kitesurf in a group. You will never go out alone plus it's so much better to have some buddies to keep an eye on you and to kite with. I think it's the people you go Kiting with that make Kitesurfing so special. Having Kitesurfing friends is also great for progression as you can show off your new moves to each other which helps to push everyone to the next level. If you are lucky enough to kite with people who are better than you then you can't help but be pulled up to their standard. When friends are watching, everyone pushes a little bit harder and comfort zones are stretched which is when the FUN starts plus progression feels amazing!"* **Stein Van Der Weiden - Big wave Kitesurfer Netherlands**

*"Be vigilant at all times"* **Ben Clarke - International Kitesurfing Instructor**

*"Having been teaching for quite some years now, I have seen my fair share of crashes, broken kites and general newbie mistakes so here's couple of*  *mega important points before I start. The "self-rescue" is one of the most important techniques any Kitesurfer can learn. Make sure you know how to self-rescue so you don't put others in danger also know that riding in shallow water is super dangerous, shallow water is the most common cause of ankle and knee injuries. So stay out of it! I would also recommend getting help from an experienced Kitesurfer before you buy anything Kitesurfing related. OK my main point is to THINK before you do. This is something I am constantly drilling into my students. THINK, do I have enough space for this jump? THINK, should I pass this Kitesurfer upwind or downwind? THINK, is my kite ready and safe to launch? Even the pros do this! Lastly make sure you have a ridiculously good time! The feeling you get when you come in and say to your mates "I just had the best session of my life" is pretty hard to beat! So get out there and enjoy! See you on the water!"* **Seb Gyde – International Kitesurfing Instructor**

*"Go out into nature and have fun as much as possible but never underestimate the massive power of the element of water."* **Marc Haendel Mallorca Spain, Kitesurfing Yacht Broker www.oceanindependance.com**

*"A great point that helped me and may well help you is about the de-power/trim system as it always confused me because many people told me to trim the de-power system to stop my kite back stalling in light wind and then I saw that some Kitesurfers had their de-power system on full power. I thought being fully powered must be for more experienced riders and de-power was for beginners but that is simply not the case. Learn how to use your trim system"* **Ben Northover International Kitesurfing Photographer bennorthover.com**

"Your first purchase should be a decent wetsuit"
**Rob Spickett International Kitesurfing Sound Engineer rsblu.co.uk**

So you think you can kite? Not yet. So be nice, humble and aware of what's going on around you! You still have a lot to learn…"
**Heike Bielek - International Kitesurfing Instructor**

*"Get some equipment as quickly as possible and get out there. Once you have your kit and are getting out on the water you will likely have the urge to start performing some jumps and tricks. Whilst this is a must to progress - take some time to just enjoy the ride and simplicity of what you are doing. If you can take a moment to not concentrate on that next jump, you may*  *find that the best part of Kitesurfing is not really thinking at all. When you can experience that blissful silence - that can be the greatest Kitesurfing experience (even if you can't get that back loop right just yet☺)"* **Jamie Fenton - Kitesurfing dentist, London fentondental.co.uk**

*Perfect what you have already learnt before moving on……"*
**Gordon Jessop Kitesurfing School Teacher UK**

*"Get advice from a knowledgeable and experienced instructor*  *when buying your first Kitesurfing gear"* **Steve Sinnhuber – International** *Kitesurfing* **Instructor learntokitesurf.co.uk**

*"Practice your self-rescue and don't take it for granted! The self-rescue and pack down is a mighty skill to have in your pocket. If done properly, the way you were taught, it will most definitely get you out of some sticky situations in the early stages of your kiting years. If you practice it and know what your doing out there it will be smooth, conserving energy and give you the confidence to know you can get out of a less than ideal situation. If done incorrectly you could find yourself in a rats nest of lines and potentially turn a bad day into a horror show.*

*My self-rescue got me out a potentially bad day and saved me a trip on the National Sea Rescue boat. Thanks goes to my instructor for drilling in into my head and making me a hell of a lot more confident out there!"* **Dan Simon – Kitesurfing health and safety officer on a super yacht somewhere really nice.**

*"One thing that sticks out for me, that I always tell my students when they are ready to head out by themselves, is to either buddy up or TELL SOMEONE where you are going and set a time limit. I feel this is really important but also KNOW YOUR LIMITS - this is a biggie. Yes, enjoy yourself, but set realistic goals, People that don't know their own capabilities and when to stop cause accidents. It's supposed to be fun, not terrifying for yourself and others."* **Molly Parr – International Kitesurfing Instructor Camber sands UK**

*"Now is when the fun really begins. It's like passing your driving test and your mum doesn't have to sit in the car anymore; the learning really begins when you have to do it by yourself. A great sense of freedom comes across you. The beautiful thing about kitesurfing is that it takes you to places far and wide and even locally that you would never have explored before. You become part of a family, Kitesurfer's are not known for being territorial, it's a nice feeling turning up at a new spot sharing a passion with someone who may not speak the same language as you; but you can smile and understand each other's happiness that day and in that place. Learning to Kitesurf gives you a new outlook on life. Before you've learnt to kite, a bad day probably consists of rain and wind. Now, this is another good day! If it's rainy it doesn't matter, you're going in the sea! If it's windy, then it couldn't be better! Be brave, don't be put off by the challenge, the greatest thrills in life don't come easily. Hope to see you ripping on the water soon. Hannah X"* **Hannah Whitely - Pro Kitesurfer, extreme sports athlete and model hannahwhiteley.com bestkiteboarding.com**

*"Practice , practice and practice. After having learnt the basics, you'll get to a stage in which you just need to go to the water and ride. Ride as much as possible. You have to get used to it, the gestures must become natural and fluid and the performance will become better and better every session. One day you'll get to the point in which you'll consider yourself a pro, but remember to never underestimate the risks that our sport involves. Never think that you are so good, nothing will happen to you. Think twice before do something. Check the conditions, the spot, the wind, the rocks, the obstacles ... A good rider is the one who spends enough time on the beach checking everything around him, who controls his gear and takes care of it in the best way, who listens to the others to learn from their experience. That's what I've learnt from my career as a rider and as a teacher, it is what I want to pass to all the new entries in this amazing discipline."* **MITU MONTEIRO – Wave Kitesurfing world championF-onekites.com**

# Bonus Chapter .......

## A Kitesurfing visualisation

**Visualising, auto suggestion and mental rehearsal can work miracles, Period. There are countless studies that prove this.**

You will see athletes mentally rehearsing what they are about to do before they perform and just about every sports or business person visualises their desired outcome and how they will achieve it.

The main benefit of visualisation is that you can practice without moving a muscle and it will have a huge positive effect on learning anything new.
This bonus chapter and specific visualisation is about how to launch your kite, ride off, stop and ride back.

It is recommended that visualisation is best practiced first thing in the morning and at the end of the day just before bed as well as before Kitesurfing.

## Before you start the guided visualisation
- Watch people Kitesurfing. This can be in real life or on YouTube and it is an important part of the visualisation. You must have a basic understanding of how to Kitesurf and be able to see what to do in your mind.

- Use positive language. Avoid thinking or saying out loud negative statements that begin with "I always" or "I never". Whatever you want to do, say that you can do it, and you will, even if it sounds like a lie to begin with!

Visualisation is sometimes known as the theatre of the mind because your task is to project a detailed image of yourself doing whatever it is that you want to do. But It's not just about images, you also need to try to feel what it will be like and how you will feel when you are Kitesurfing.

**Warning! Do not drive or operate machinery while reading or listening to this!**

Find a quiet space where you won't be disturbed for ten minutes or more and sit comfortably, as comfortably as possible.

So now you are sitting comfortably its time to now relax. Really relax. Breathe deeply. Close your eyes. Spend a few moments to relax and clear your mind. As you sit back or lay down and relax you are going to loosen all your muscles.Start by thinking about relaxing your feet, feel them go warm as they loosen and relax, then relax your calf muscles, relax your thighs, now relax your hips, feel the weight of your body as you relax even more. Now relax your stomach muscles, relax your back, relax your chest, relax your arms, your hands and your fingers. Now relax your shoulders, your neck, your face muscles, feel the weight of your eye lids and finally relax your jaw. Sink deep into your seat. Take a deep breath.

Breathe deeply. Enjoy the deep relaxation that you are feeling and know that it is going to help you to learn how to Kitesurf.  Now imagine that you are on a warm sandy beach and the sun is out, the wind is gentle. You can hear the wind blowing the trees and feel the wind on your face. You are about to go Kitesurfing, you have set your kite up and you are ready to go. You are first going to launch your kite and you feel happy and confident that you have setup your kite correctly and you have lots of space around you.

Before you launch, you stand for a moment with your back to the perfect cross on shore wind so you can visualise your launch. As you look to your left you have the land and when you look to the right you can see the ocean. You know that you are going to launch towards the sea and ninety degrees to the wind in the safe zone. You calmly walk over to your kite. It is secured on the beach by some sand and your board is on top. You pass it to your assistant who holds it up in the C position. You remind them politely to let go when you give the thumbs up signal. As you walk calmly back to your bar, you feel calm and confident and you are looking forward to your Kitesurfing session. When you get back to your bar you hook in your safety leash and connect your chicken loop. You pull your lines out tight and walk slowly into the wind until your kite stops flapping, you check around you to make sure you have lots of space and then you give the thumbs up sign.

Your assistant lets go and you gently pull on your bar so you kite rises up a few meters into the air, nice and slowly. You pick up your board, hold it by the handle and walk into the ocean keeping your kite low in the sky. You continue to walk into the clear blue ocean until the water is up to your thighs. You check that you have lots of space around you and move your kite directly above your head to 12 o clock. You sit back in the water, put your board on your feet and relax. You are going to ride off to your right so you pull in your bar and then pull on the right side of your bar which makes your kite move down to your right, as you feel a little power, you extend your legs, lean forwards and stand up slowly.

As you stand up, you keep your kite on your right and start riding. You lean back, keeping your legs bent, your kite low and you ride further and further. You pick up some speed and can feel the rush of the wind on your face as well as hear the noise of the water rushing past your board. As you look in front of you, you can see the spray from your board trailing behind you as you glide across the water.

You are relaxed and smiling to yourself, you feel amazing, you are Kitesurfing and it feels great! You have gone out as far as you want to go so you slowly move your kite back up above your head to 12, you slow down gradually until you come to a graceful stop and you sit back in the water. You take a moment to look around you and enjoy the view of the land from the sea then you move your kite down to your left, as you feel a little power, you extend your legs, lean forwards and stand up slowly. You are now riding comfortably back to the land. When you get close, you slowly move your kite up to 12 and sit back and stop. You are back to where you started and you feel amazing, you have done it, you smile and put your hand in the air, you can ride back to where you started. Well done. Enjoy the feeling of achievement.

**Hold these images and feelings in your mind for as long as can and when you are ready its time to open your eyes, feeling refreshed and excited to go and practice.**

**Now the real fun begins....**

# The Magic Threes refresher course

**The most important part of Kitesurfing is of course The Wind.**

You must know the answers to the following three questions.

## What is the wind strength?
## What is the wind direction?
## What is the weather forecast?

### Wind strength check made simple
1. Find out the strength of the wind to make the correct choice of Kite.
2. Look at the sea, look at what kites are being used, look at an accurate wind reading, ask other Kitesurfers.
3. Avoid strong winds, stick to light winds while learning, if in doubt, don't go out.

### Wind direction check made simple
1. Stand with your back to the wind to find out the direction of the wind.
2. Cross on shore winds are the easiest and safest wind directions for Kitesurfing.
3. Never Kitesurf in any off shore winds, if in doubt don't go out.

### Forecasts, tides and wind effects made simple
1. Always check a wind, weather and tide forecast before you go Kitesurfing.
2. Remember that a forecast is just a forecast and that you must check the actual conditions at your location.
3. Talk to local Kitesurfer's for local information such as currents, wind and tide effects and remember if in doubt don't go out.

### Site check made simple
1. Always take five minutes before every Kitesurfing session to check what all the potential dangers are and decide if your location is suitable for your skill level.
2. Launch and Kitesurf as far away from any potential dangers as possible, if in doubt don't go out.
3. Shallow water is the most common cause of injury in Kitesurfing, stay in water that is above your knee.

**The wind window made simple**
1. Always stand with your back to the wind.
2. The no power zone is to your extreme left and right and above your head.
3. The power zone is in front of you and the maximum power is in front of your face.

**The Kitesurfing rights of way made simple**
1. Avoid any collisions with anything at all costs.
2. Always keep a minimum distance of two kite line lengths between you any objects.
3. Give way to all other water users.

**Set up of your kite made simple**
1. Remember to connect your pumps safety hook to your kite
2. Pump your kite up until it is hard.
3. A lose kite is a dangerous kite, always keep your kite secured with enough weight.

**Setting up your lines made simple**
1. Walk your lines out downwind and separate them all before you connect them to your kite.
2. Connect the outside lines to the outside of the kite and the centre lines to the centre of the kite.
3. Always perform a pre-flight check to make sure your lines are connected correctly and that your main safety system is working as it should.

**Emergency safety systems made simple**
1. Know that **letting go is your first and main safety** and this is the most commonly used safety system but be prepared to use your emergency safety systems at any time.
2. Know your safety systems inside out and out, know how to use them with your eyes closed and check that they are working before every session.
3. Make sure that your final safety release is attached to a fixed point to the side or the front of your harness and do not hesitate to use it if your life is in danger.

**Pre flight check made simple**
1. Always perform a pre-flight check as part of set up
2. Activate your safety to make sure it is working and is not damaged.
3. Lift up your lines individually to check that your outside lines are connected to the outside of your kite and your inner lines are connected to the inner part of the kite without twists, lines touching each other and your bridles are untwisted.

## Control of your kite made simple
1. Pull your bar in for maximum control.
2. Push your bar away to have less power and to find the sweet spot.
3. Let go of your bar in an emergency to stop the power immediately.

## Preparing to launch your kite made simple
1. Always perform a pre-flight check before you launch any kite by checking that the lines are connected correctly without twists and that your safety system works.
2. Make sure you launch at least two kite line lengths away from any dangers on the beach such as rocks, people or any hard objects.
3. Plan to launch your kite so you are facing the sea if it is not possible to launch your kite while standing in the water.

## Launching your Kitesurfing kite made simple
1. Walk into the wind until your kite stops flapping at 90 degrees to the wind direction.
2. Check that a bridle hasn't twisted over the wing tip.
3. Be gentle with your bar, be prepared to let go immediately if something goes wrong and get into the water as soon as possible

## Basic flying of your Kitesurfing kite made simple
1. Practice basic flying in water above your knee and below your waist so you can stand up and do not drift downwind.
2. Be gentle with the bar, you can control your kite using your fingertips.
3. Pull the bar in for control, push the bar away for less power and let go when you crash your kite.

## Flying your kite with one hand made simple
1. If your kite is on your left, hold your bar with your right hand and if your kite is on your right, hold your kite with your left hand.
2. Hold your bar near the centre but not in the centre.
3. When flying with one hand remember that if you push your bar away, your kite goes down and if you pull your bar in and your kite goes up.

## Relaunching your Kitesurfing kite from the water made simple
1. Untwist your lines before you start the launch.
2. Pull gently and aim to launch at the edge of the wind window where there is the least power.
3. Launch your kite towards the land if you have the choice so you don't get pulled out to sea.

## Body dragging made simple
1. You go where your kite goes, keep your kite in one area by making small focused power strokes.
2. Keep your kite low in the wind window around **10** or **2** to move easily to your left or right.
3. To stop, slowly move your kite to **12.**

## Board recovery made simple
1. Aim to keep your kite low at **10** or **2** and drags 10-20 meters in each direction.
2. Stay more on your front and not so much on your side.
3. Change direction slowly, move your kite over your head and through **12** using small gentle movements of your bar.

## Board start preparations made simple
1. Practice balance body dragging before your board starts.
2. You must have the wind directly on your back before you start.
3. To stop in a controlled manor, bring your kite to **12** or simply let go in an emergency.

## Board start theory made simple
1. Build the power slowly, be extremely cautious.
2. If you try but cannot stand up, stop and start from the beginning of the process.
3. Aim to get to the level where you keep your kite in the air after each attempt because you are building the power gradually.

## Putting your board on made simple
1. Put your board on in the same way every time regardless of what direction you will be riding so it becomes an unconscious and easy habit.
2. Hold your board by the handle, sit back in the water and take your feet off the ground, remember to put your board on as it will not magically float onto your feet.
3. If you hold your kite with your right hand, hold your board handle with your left hand and put your right foot in first as quickly as you can without pulling on your bar.

## The board start made simple
1. Wind on your back, check the area in front of you is clear so you know it is safe to start.
2. Kite to **1** if you are boardstarting to your left or **11** if you are starting to your right, pull your bar in.
3. Dive your kite down in the direction you want to go, lean forwards, extend your legs, stand up.

## Controlling your speed when you are up on your board made simple

### In the following order, to speed up
1. Pull your bar in all the way.
2. Move your kite aggressively back into the power by pulling hard on your opposite hand to the direction you are traveling in.
3. Come off your edge by leaning forwards and turn your front hip towards the kite. This will point your board towards the pull of the kite and you will require less power to keep riding.

### In the following order, to slow down
1. Push the bar away from your body and keep your bar pushed out until you slow down.
2. Keep or move your kite lower in the wind window to at least **10** or **2** so you can lean back.
3. Apply more pressure in your heels and lean back so you can edge harder and turn your head away from your kite and look over your shoulder.

### Riding upwind made simple
1. Make sure you have plenty of power so you can keep your kite low and hold it at 10 or 2 without moving it.
2. Ride slowly, control your speed by pulling your bar in or pushing it way, change direction slowly by moving your kite slowly through 12 to the new direction.
3. Pick a point a long way upwind, turn your head towards it, lean back and straighten your front leg slightly.

### Walking with your kite on the land made simple
1. If your kite is on your left, hold your board with your left hand and control your kite with your right hand and the opposite if your kite is on your right.
2. Keep your kite low, below **11** or **1** while walking on the land
3. Be prepared to let go immediately if you are pulled

### Self-Landing made simple
1. Before you self-land make sure you have at least two kite line lengths of clear space downwind of you.
2. Move your kite to the edge of the wind window either at **9** or **3** and activate your safety.
3. Pull yourself back to your kite up the one safety line using the hand over hand technique, do not touch your bar throughout the whole self-land and continue up the safety line until you have your kite in your hands.

## Trimming your kite made simple
1. Make sure you understand how your kites depower system works before you fly it.
2. Shorter centre lines mean less power and longer centre lines mean more power.
3. Most kites fly best with a little depower.

## Changing direction made simple
1. Practice sliding turns by coming to a controlled stop and then board starting in the opposite direction as soon as you stop.
2. Bring your kite slowly back to **12** and slow right down.
3. Board start in the new direction just before you sink and ride off slightly downwind before leaning back, edging and riding back in the same direction

## Self-Rescue and deep water pack down made simple
1. Avoid a self-rescue by conducting and effective wind and site assessment every time you go Kitesurfing. Avoid marginal conditions, If in doubt, don't go out.
2. Release your safety, wind your safety line around the end of your bar, lock off your safety line, wind yourself back to your kite, turn your kite over, hold a bridle, bend your kite over into a **C** shape position and face the land.
3. Only perform a full pack down if you have no other way of getting back to the land.

## Light wind riding made simple
1. Know that in light wind your kite should be setup for low power and be depowered, yes less power.
2. Know that the wind window is smaller in light winds and your kite can drop out of the sky from any lower than **11** or **1**.
3. Focus on keeping your kite in the air as relaunching in light wind can be impossible, remember that your kite is the most important component of Kitesurfing, keep it moving or down loop it if is falling out of the sky.

## Light wind relaunching made simple
1. Aim to launch your kite towards the land if safe to do so otherwise you may drift out to sea, If you cannot launch on one side then try launching on the other side.
2. Launch more in front of you in the power zone where your kite will catch the wind the most and be extremely gentle when pulling on your steering line as your kite leaves the water.
3. If you cannot relaunch be prepared to self-rescue.

## Back stalling made simple
1. Remember to set your kite and trim system up for less power to prevent back stalling in light wind.
2. As soon as your kite falls backwards push your bar away.
3. Fly your kite back up to 12 as soon as possible

## Down looping your kite made simple
1. Only down loop your kite as a last resort when you are on the water with at least 2 kite lines distance between you and any objects. Downloop when it is at the edge of the wind window where there is less power
2. If your kite is on your right pull hard on the right side of your bar, if your kite is on your left, pull hard on the left side of your bar.
3. Do not twist your bar, keep it level and keep pulling hard until your kite turns all the way around

## Hot launching made simple
1. Only hot launch when you are in the water.
2. You cannot hot launch unless the leading edge of your kite is facing directly towards **12**.
3. Push your bar away and pull on your centre lines or depower rope if needed

## Dealing with an inverted kite made simple
1. Pump your kite up extremely hard to help prevent an invert.
2. If you are in deep water you can fly your kite inverted and body drag with your board back to shallow water or to the land.
3. Activate your main safety and then reactivate it usually fixes the invert, if not, land or self-land your kite and be prepared to self rescue.

## Twisted lines made simple
1. You can fly your kite with twisted lines as long as your bar is the right way round.
2. Get back to the land as soon as you can and land your kite to untwist your lines.
3. Activate your main safety and self-rescue if your lines become tangled and your kite is not flying properly.

## Putting your safety back together under tension made simple
1. Use the palms down, thumbs out, hand over hand method to get back to your safety system making sure you stay upwind of your lines so you do not get any body parts or equipment  tangled in your safety line.
2. Do not hold on to your bar or safety system as your kite will power up, consider wrapping your safety line around your spreader bar hook to help make putting your safety back together more easy.
3. When your safety is back together feed the safety line back through as slowly as possible.

### The death loop made simple
1. Check that your bridles are not twisted around your wing tips when launching.
2. Know that activating your main safety is the first thing to do if you experience a death loop, know how to activate your safety system and how to get to your line cutter with your eyes closed.
3. If your main safety will not activate, you can force a back stall and stop the death loop by pulling hard on a steering line, preferably the one furthest away from you.

### Buying equipment made simple
1. Invest as much as you can in your equipment but you can get quality second hand gear from a reputable shop.
2. The quality of your equipment has a direct impact on the quality of your Kitesurfing experience as well as the speed of your progression.
3. Your Kite is the most important piece of equipment followed by your personal protective gear and lastly your board. Make your purchase decisions based on where you will Kitesurf the most.

### Equipment maintenance made simple
1. Check all your equipment for any signs of wear such as knots in the lines, tears in your kite and fraying lines ropes or pigtails. Repair or replace immediately. Tighten up your board screws every week.
2. Don't pack your kite away if it is wet or has any sand on it and never leave your kite in the sun for more than 15 minutes or flapping in the wind longer than absolutely necessary.
3. Rinse and dip if possible, all other equipment with fresh water after each session making sure all sand has been removed.

# I hope that you have enjoyed reading Learn Kitesurfing Faster and that you take what you have learned and practice safely.

# Just to remind you to get the most value out of your purchase...

**Listen to the podcast** Toms Kiteboarding Tips
(on Apple and Spotify) and get a refresher on the way to the beach
(and hopefully be entertained too!)

**Follow** Toms Kiteboarding Tips
on Instagram and on Facebook for regular tips

Join the Learn Kitesurfing Faster Facebook group and get support from the
community.

Please feel free to get in contact with me and ask any kitesurfing related
question through Instagram / Facebook / email
tom@tomskiteboardingtips.com

Visit www.tomskiteboardingtips.com
and read the blog
Check out the Youtube channel
Toms Kiteboarding Tips

Learn Kitesurfing Faster is available on Audiobook format from Amazons Audible

Learn Kitesurfing Faster is available in French and German on Amazon

Come and have a personal lesson or advanced coaching session with me in the
ultimate Kitesurfing paradise that Im lucky enough to call home in the Turks and
Caicos islands @thebigbluecollective

Lastly huge THANK YOU to all the people who have taken the time to get in
contact or left a review over the years since this book was first published in 2017
also for all the lovely reviews on Amazon as every single one are hugely
appreciated and it means a lot to me.

If you would be so kind to take a few moments of your precious time to leave a
review on Amazon I would be eternally grateful as it really helps the book and all
the other kitesurfing resources I have created, to help more people practice safe
and respectful kitesurfing as well as spreading more good vibes on the beach.

Made in United States
Troutdale, OR
07/24/2024

21522065R00090